Secret
Spirit

Secret Spirit

SALLY MORGAN

MARDLE

First published in 2021 by Mardle Books
15 Church Road
London, SW13 9HE

www.mardlebooks.com

Text © 2021 Sally Morgan

Paperback ISBN 9781914451201
eBook ISBN 9781914451263

A CIP catalogue record for this book is available from the British Library.

Every reasonable effort has been made to trace copyright-holders of material
reproduced in this book, but if any have been inadvertently overlooked the
publishers would be glad to hear from them.

Printed in the UK

10 9 8 7 6 5 4 3 2 1

Dedicated to His Lordship, John;
my love, my life, my world.

Fly high my darling, I know you
will be forever walking by my side.

Always in my heart.

Contents

Introduction

The world has changed, and it will never go back to the way it was before.

That sounds like a scary statement, doesn't it? But don't worry. Change isn't a bad thing.

People are incredibly adaptable, even those who think they aren't. Sometimes you just have to look at things from a different perspective. And life is rarely as simple as good and bad, or black and white. So, there are lots of things to be thankful for in this 'new normal'. With more people working from home now, hands up who will miss cramming onto public transport for the morning commute, being crushed between someone with bad breath and someone with bad hygiene? Thought not. Or how about all the social engagements you've been able to get out of by blaming 'the situation'?

We've all re-evaluated what's important in life and generally it boils down to a few core things; security, health and loved ones. As long as we've got these, and enough toilet paper and tinned food (if the early days of the pandemic were anything to go by), we are generally okay. If the pandemic showed us one thing, it is that life doesn't have to be so complicated and busy. Of course, it's lovely to be able to go out, to have some freedom, to travel and go on holiday, but as long as we have our health, our loved ones around us and enough money to pay the bills, buy food and make the occasional random Amazon purchase, we can survive, thrive and find happiness. The rest are luxuries.

The big lessons many of us learned, are that we are more adaptable than we previously believed and that we rely on people who were previously invisible to us (think delivery drivers, supermarket workers, nurses and care workers). We also learned that kindness is a gift and a blessing and it makes the world go round.

Something quite incredible has happened since those first news reports broke in early 2020 about a strange new virus spreading through a city in China that few of us had heard of. There's been a collective awakening. So many terrible things have happened, so many people have lost their lives and lost loved ones. The tragedy has been on an almost unimaginable scale, but with it we have seen amazing acts of love, kindness and compassion. From the international-level gestures of rich nations helping poor nations with vaccines, to the individual acts of love between neighbours and strangers who have reached out to each other to help the elderly and isolated. Then there were the collective acts of support as thousands stood on doorsteps each Thursday night, clapping and banging pots and pans to show appreciation for the heroic NHS workers, battling to save lives.

It will take many years for us all to come to terms with events, to absorb and process it all and make sense of it. It will take even longer to work out where the virus came from and find ways to stop something similar happening again. Inevitably, the passage of time will dull memories and as we get used to living with the virus we'll return to lives similar to those we led before. We'll start to travel again, but will be a bit more cautious in the future. Offices will start to fill again, but will not be as busy as before because people will work from home several days a week.

So, while things may feel the same, there will be subtle differences. For one, I predict that masks will remain quite a common sight for a long time to come, if not permanently. People will continue wearing them now – much as they have done in South-East Asia for many years, where, on public transport and in busy shopping centres, they are commonplace. Remember how weird and alien they looked when the first people started wearing them in 2020, or how you'd give Asian tourists a second glance when you saw them wearing face coverings before the pandemic. Now we understand why they are a good idea.

Social distancing is also here to stay to some extent. People will be much more aware of personal space and much less likely to want to put themselves in situations where they are crammed into enclosed spaces.

These changes are obvious. There are, however, more subtle changes that aren't immediately obvious but that will still have an impact on the way we live our lives. These are the changes in behaviour and awareness that affect the way we interact with each other. On a visible level, there will be less handshaking and more namaste hand gestures. On a deeper level, the world, I hope, will be a kinder and more caring place. Greater emphasis will be given to mental health. As individuals we will be more aware of our own mental health, and as communities, we will be more aware of the mental health of others and the behaviours we exhibit that can affect this.

An appreciation and greater awareness of mental health has helped people get through the pandemic.

Introduction

People understand much more now how things like loneliness, anxiety and depression are just as damaging to health as viruses. In a way, they are a kind of virus themselves, and by helping neighbours, listening to people who are suffering and talking about mental health more, we are on the way to developing cures. Mental health is not a taboo subject anymore and that's a very good thing. We have mental health ambassadors now, like Prince Harry, of whom his mum, Princess Diana, one of my former clients, would have been very proud.

The Princess of Wales was ahead of her time when it came to discussing mental health. More than anyone she understood how destructive depression and anxiety are. She used to tell me how certain people in the royal household would change the subject whenever she tried to talk about how she felt and how difficult she found living in what she believed was the gilded cage of royalty. She explained how, as a royal, you were expected to brush those kinds of feelings under the carpet.

When I watched Harry and Meghan's interview with Oprah Winfrey, I got chills. It was like watching history repeat itself. It would be tempting to think that things don't change, but on the positive side they do, because generally we now accept that mental health is something that needs to be nurtured and taken care of, and by sticking their heads above the royal parapet and talking about it, Harry and Meghan are helping drive the debate forward.

People say that there is a mental health epidemic since the pandemic, and it is true that there are those who have suffered loss, ill health, isolation and anxiety as a result of the global health crisis. There will be millions who need help finding their equilibrium again. But there are just as many who would have been struggling before, and who have been able to talk about it because the conversation has opened.

People are searching for answers and for healing. There has been a huge emotional reset in the world. We've had a collective shock that has shaken us to our core and made us reconsider life in a way that we haven't since the end of the Second World War. We haven't yet started to understand the long-term metaphysical effects the pandemic will have on us. Generally, it will be positive. People will be more aware of their impact on others, both on a practical health level and on an emotional level. People want answers, they want hope and for the millions who have lost loved ones, they want reassurance that those who have passed are at peace.

And that's where people like me come in. I am a medium, or psychic. In the old days I would probably have been called a witch and burned alive or put in a spiky barrel and rolled down a hill. Thankfully the world is a bit more enlightened and forgiving nowadays and instead I'm called upon to connect the living with the dead, or, to be more specific, to connect the living with the spirit energy of those who have passed into the realm beyond the one we live in. It is a place that feeds us and guides us. Which all sounds slightly mad, I know. But trust me on this, it makes a lot of sense and, if you can harness this spirit power and so live a more spiritual life, good things happen.

Given the events since 2020, and the way the world has changed, people are understandably seeking a deeper connection to their spirituality because they're scared and want reassurance. We've all had a very sudden and unwelcome introduction to our mortality. Humans are great at getting on with things, preoccupying ourselves with our day-to-day lives and generally ignoring the fact that one day, we'll all die. No one wants to be reminded of that do they? And then, bang! Suddenly something happens and every one of us gets a rather horrific wake-up call to remind us that we are fallible, vulnerable and, in the scheme of things, quite insignificant. It's like a freezing cold shower for the mind. A proper shock to the system to sober us up. And now we need to look for deeper meaning and are forced to investigate the sometimes uncomfortable truth.

The good news is that there really isn't anything to be frightened of. Life can be full of meaning and well-lived and death isn't the end. It is merely a transit point to a better reality, like Crewe Station, but with better facilities and a nicer first-class lounge.

I sat down to write this book as life began to restart, because I realised that so many people were looking for answers and needed to try to understand what had happened to themselves and their loved ones on a spiritual level.

Science and the news can only tell us so much. We can find out that the virus came from a bat or leaked from a lab. We can follow its trajectory across the globe, track its variants, deconstruct its genome and create vaccines. But on a personal level, answers are harder to find.

Will I be okay?

How can I be strong?

How do I cope with the loss I've suffered?

Where is my life going?

What does the future hold?

These are all much more perplexing and subjective questions.

Introduction

I hope that in the following pages I'll be able to give you some answers, and if I can't give you the answers, I can give you guidance on how to find those answers, because when it comes to spirit energy, I can guide and explain, but ultimately, it's up to you to find it in yourself because everybody can access their hidden powers, which are innate – they are naturally in us all.

Spirit energy resides in us all and connects us to the universe. Don't get me wrong. I know this can sound a bit woo-woo when you hear it for the first time, but believe me, it's the truth. Inside us all there is a ball of spiritual energy, like a glowing Duracell, packed full of power. Most people only ever use a fraction of it. This book is about the secret of that spirit energy, how to tap into it and how to harness your own spirituality. We get so much from it. It radiates love and hope.

As a medium I have this innate ability to be able to connect with you, even though you're sitting there and perhaps not even talking to me. Once you understand the secret of your spirit power, the possibilities are immense. I hope that by sharing my secret with you I can give you peace of mind, strength and a glimpse into another wondrous world.

Chapter 1

Changes

The good news is that you don't have to be a fanatically religious person. I'm certainly not. You don't have to believe in a god with a flowing beard, or miracles or biblical stories. There are literally millions of people in the world who have had some kind of experience or event that they would describe as spiritual or supernatural and who are not religious at all. Likewise, many religious people will also have had experiences that are other-worldly and unexplainable and which they will attribute to their religion. Religions have, after all, got a vested interest in the afterlife, but often their interpretations change because of historic or ecumenical factors.

For example, in Medieval Catholic Europe ghosts were assumed to be the tormented souls of people suffering for their sins in purgatory. But during the Protestant

Reformation, since most Protestants believed that souls went immediately to heaven or hell, paranormal activity was instead thought to be the work of angels, demons or other supernatural beings. It was all about historical context.

Today, belief in orthodox religions is on the decline in the West, but beliefs in spirits and the supernatural are as popular as ever. For example, a 2019 poll found that more than four out of 10 Americans believed that ghosts or demons exist and over a third said they had felt the presence of a ghost or spirit.

When it comes to ghosts, Mormons and Roman Catholics are the most believing religions, with 57 per cent of followers of both denominations expressing a belief, while 52 per cent of Muslims were also likely to say they believe that ghosts definitely or probably exist. Such beliefs are equally popular in Britain, where people are more likely to believe in ghosts than a divine creator. Believe me, the truth about spirit is fantastic enough. All you need is curiosity and to know that there is an energy field that connects everything and that will accept your own personal ball of spirit energy when it's time for you to go. But more of that later.

* * *

Changes

This is the beginning and we'll be taking the journey together.

I started to really investigate spirit energy about a decade ago, after a lifetime of being a medium. I've always had what they call 'the gift' and it had led me along my path in life, as it does all of us. We all have the ability to use this gift of energy; we just need to be shown how. But as I got older, I wanted to understand more about what was happening to me when I performed psychic readings and what was happening to the people I read for (variously called receivers or sitters).

When I started touring my show in theatres, I became even more fascinated by the ability I had. Where did it come from? What was causing it? What strange power allowed me to connect with the spirits of people's loved ones and see aspects of their lives and futures that I couldn't possibly have known in advance? It is an incredible phenomenon and one I was desperate to learn more about. My level of understanding began to grow deeper and deeper. I started looking at what I was doing differently. I took a more objective approach, which at first seemed bizarre as I had always been someone who had bags of empathy and had always invested emotionally in my work and the people I met. I still maintained that emotional link with the audience and the people I was reading for, but after the shows I started to make notes about what had happened and thought about theories that might explain the seemingly unexplainable.

The pandemic put a stop to my theatre shows and, like the rest of the working world, I went online and started doing video readings. I also increasingly shared my gift through social media. What I discovered was surprising. I could still connect with the spirit energy of the people I was talking to, even though we were not in the same room. Often, we weren't even in the same country. Yet the information and messages I received came through loud and clear. My spirit energy Wi-Fi was like superfast broadband, and none of the spirits I picked up came through on mute.

As the months went on, thousands of people got in touch looking for reassurance and answers. I did hundreds of Zoom readings and realised that the world was desperate for some spiritual healing.

Now, with the benefit of hindsight, I think it's safe to say that as a world we have become more spiritual. The pandemic asked questions of us that previously we chose to ignore. It might sound dramatic, but I truly believe we are on the horizon of a golden age of spirituality where each culture in its own way will endeavour to lead a more spiritual life.

Changes

All through my life, spirit has guided and helped me. It has led me to make decisions that have opened amazing possibilities. It's protected me and, in some cases, exposed me to risk, but eventually always led me back to the path I was destined to take in life. It's been my true north and my guiding star. It's been there for me through thick and thin and now I want to share its secrets with you.

* * *

A connection to spirit energy is different for different people. For me, as a medium, my connection is strong and allows me the ability to link to the spirit energy of others. For people who are just starting out on their journey, strengthening spirit energy will have a different effect at first. They will find themselves happier and calmer until, eventually, they'll start to develop the ability to recognise the signs from the world beyond this one.

It's hard to describe what a psychic connection feels like because I believe it's different for different people. For me it starts with flashes of images and a feeling that something is building up in my mind. It's not pressure, it's a lovely feeling, like a gentle buzz in the back of my mind, like a single light bulb in a silent room. I can hear it in my head but it's not quite noise, more like a current of electricity. The images could be anything, faces, buildings, scenes from someone else's life. And they come with emotions, usually love, sometimes tinged with other things, like sadness or laughter. For me, this is how the process begins. I open myself to it and invite it in and as the energy builds, the images come into focus and get sharper. My field of vision sometimes blurs and softens at the edges. In my mind I hear sounds and voices, sometimes I experience smells and touch. Every reading is different because every spirit is different. Each one I connect to is, or was, an individual. This is how it's always been since I was a little girl and had my first psychic encounter. I've always had the ability to see things that other people don't.

It took me many years to understand what it was and how to harness it. When I was really young, I couldn't control it. It was my other world, my other reality, and the two existed simultaneously, which meant I'd often be at school in lessons sitting with my classmates and the souls of the dearly departed at the same time in the same space. It took me a few years to realise which was which, and to try to keep the two separate.

On occasions, when I'd blurt out some exclamation or other because I caught sight of something unpleasant in the spirit world in the corner of my eye, the teacher would assume I was being disruptive and shut me in the supply cupboard. This was fine by me, because Ken lived in the supply cupboard. He was the school's former caretaker and had committed suicide in the Victorian era. I looked forward to our chats. My childhood was a real-life version of Rent-a-Ghost, full of jump-scares, disembodied voices and unlikely characters who had the disconcerting habit of fading in and out of focus.

Today, thankfully, I can tune in and out of this constant otherworld that buzzes in the back of my mind like a swarm of bees and generally I can turn it off completely when I need get on with life on the Earth plane. But every so often, the energy that drives the spirits in this place is so strong it barges into my mind. Some readings I do for others are so emotionally charged, so full of love or sorrow that I can't close myself off or control them, and instead I have to surrender and feel everything.

This was the case several weeks into the first UK lockdown, in May 2020, when I logged on to my computer to give a reading for a woman called Pam who had contacted me the week before and booked in a session. It had taken me a few weeks to get up to speed with Zoom and if I'm honest, initially, I was sceptical. I had done telephone readings in the past and they were always good but for the previous 10 years I had been touring, taking my show to theatres around the country and doing readings for hundreds of people at a time. The energy and responses I received were amazing and, in my opinion, sustained the link between spirit, me and the audience. It was a cumulative effect. The more people, the more spirits and the more intense the energy in the room, which led to better connections and messages. It was a feedback loop. I was so used to working this way with big crowds, I didn't know if I could go back to basics like in the old days when I ran my mediumship practice from the front office of my suburban semi in Surrey, like Whoopi Goldberg in *Ghost*.

But then Pam appeared on the screen and I felt a jolt of energy that almost made me drop the glass of water I was holding.

Immediately, in my mind's eye, I felt the image of a man. He was old, around 80, rather overweight, with kind eyes that shone out from his face. Sometimes I just get the blurry image of a face, or the outline of a person; other times the messages come with a whole panoply of extra information. It could be smells, sounds or background images. In this gentleman's case I could smell disinfectant and hear a slow, rhythmic pumping sound, like bellows being inflated at regular intervals. Inhale, exhale.

Changes

In many cases I also experience some of what the person in spirit was experiencing towards the end of their life. I assume it's like a residue that stays with them for a time after they pass. Over the years I've got used to this, even though it's not always a pleasant thing to feel, particularly if the person in spirit met a painful or unpleasant end. When I was young this could be distressing, like that time when I was working as a dental nurse and I suddenly felt the presence of a woman standing over me who had obviously died from crush injuries sustained in some kind of car accident. There was a male patient in the chair who was under anaesthetic, and the spirit was a close relative who had no doubt decided to keep an eye on him while he underwent root canal treatment. I could feel her looking intently at him from behind me and I carried on with my work as if nothing was happening. By that point in my life, I'd learned not to discuss what I was experiencing from the spirit world, especially in day-to-day life, for fear of being locked up. In this case however it became increasingly difficult to put our ethereal visitor to the back of my mind, because the more intense her concentration on the patient became, the more I experienced an uncomfortable pressure on my chest.

As the dentist drilled and gouged his way deeper into the patient's molars, the pain in my chest increased and I had to try very hard to control my breathing. I know the woman meant no harm and she was there because she loved and cared for the man in the chair (who made a full recovery), but in a strange way the manner of her death seemed to hang around her like a faint shadow. It didn't seem to bother her in the slightest, by the way. When we pass, the pain goes. But someone like me, attuned to the information held within spirit energy, can sometimes physically experience what that information tells me. I hope that makes sense. Perhaps another way to describe it is that spirits and their energy are in part like digital data. They hold memories and feelings in the form of information, which is formless in its purest manifest-ation, but which, when interpreted by a computer, i.e. a medium, is translated into physical and emotional elements, such as feelings and memories.

So, back to Pam, her Zoom reading, the elderly gentleman and the pumping bellows. As his energy grew and his image became clearer in my mind, I also started to feel my breath become shallow. It wasn't uncomfortable or painful, and it was momentary, but definitely pronounced.

"Why do I feel like I am struggling to breathe?" I asked Pam.

Given what was going on in the world at the time I knew the answer before Pam confirmed it. The gentleman had died of Covid. It was my first experience of Covid loss. Sadly, since then, it has become a familiar feature to my work.

"Oh, you poor love," I said to Pam. "He got Covid didn't he? It was so quick."

Pam was blinking back tears and nodded her head in affirmation.

"He was your dad," I said.

She nodded again.

There was such a strong bond between the two it was obvious to me that they were father and daughter. I'd felt the same kind of pull thousands of times before. From spirit I was receiving broken images of a life of love lived together, a babe in the arms of a beaming, proud father, a child on a bicycle wobbling away from the steadying hands of her father, a graduation, a family holiday, a grown woman in tears comforted in the embrace of her dad. The man was showing me his life. And mixed in with all these images and emotions there was someone else. I could feel her, too.

"Is your mum in spirit, too?" I frowned. It wasn't immediately clear because the link between Pam and her father was so solid and clear, but in the periphery of my mind I could sense another energy source growing in strength. As it got stronger, I started to see the outline of an elderly female face, soft-lined and smiling. As she came into focus, I could see she was the spitting image of Pam.

And once again I felt the tightness in my lungs.

"Oh my God," I gasped, unconsciously putting my hand on my heart and inhaling deeply, "your mum died of Covid too, didn't she?"

Pam explained everything.

Her dad had been a victim of the first wave and had succumbed to the virus in mid-April, 2020. He was 83 and even though he was fit, he was no match for the disease. He had a temperature and shortness of breath for several days which got worse until he was taken into hospital on a Friday afternoon and placed on a venti-lator the following morning. By Monday he was dead. Meanwhile, his wife, who had recovered from cancer three years before, also contracted the virus and was taken into hospital shortly after her husband.

"They were both in the same ward, unconscious and on ventilators. We couldn't go in and see them," Pam explained through her tears. Her grief was palpable.

By now the information was flowing through me. I could feel an unbreakable bond of love between the two spirits. I knew they had been married for a very long time and were so close they were almost one being. That's one of the beautiful things about true love. Obviously, the fireworks that go off at the start of a relationship are great and exciting, but when they fizzle out, which they always do, they are replaced by something much more valuable. True love is an indestructible glue and when we find it, it lasts a lifetime and keeps us together into the afterlife.

"They were married so long," I told her, "they knew everything about each other and they loved you and your brother so much." I had worked out from what I was feeling that Pam had a sibling.

"We begged the hospital to let us in, just to say goodbye," said Pam. "The nurses held up an iPad and let us speak to them, but by then they were both on ventilators and in comas. They had tubes down their mouths and all we could hear was the sound of the machines."

Pam's immense grief was mixed with frustration and anger.

"I never had the chance to tell them how much I love them. I never had the chance to say goodbye," she sobbed. "I can't bear the thought that they died alone, hooked up to machines."

The waves of love I was receiving from the couple in spirit were intense. They didn't want their daughter to suffer.

"They know how much you love them darling," I soothed. "They want you to know they are at peace and in a beautiful place and that they hear you when you speak to them."

"I talk to them all the time," Pam smiled through her tears.

"And they want you to know that they didn't die alone, they were together. When your mum passed, your dad was there waiting for her. You don't have to feel angry. They are together now and always will be."

* * *

Since that first Covid reading, the numbers increased almost daily, to the point that a year into the pandemic and I was receiving daily requests for video readings from people who had lost loved ones to the virus. Most of them followed a similar theme. The first thing anyone who has suffered the loss of a loved one wants to know is whether their loved one is okay and at peace.

They always are, because when we pass, we go to a place of love.

The other common themes I noticed were frustration and helplessness from the bereaved, and sometimes anger. This is understandable given the nature of the deaths, especially in the first wave when it was such a new disease and doctors were still trying to find the best ways to treat it.

There was a lot of fear in the world and fear does strange things to people. Scared people don't think straight. And when we're scared and don't understand things, we start to look for answers in unlikely places. That's why, in my opinion, so many people have become obsessed with conspiracy theories. They look for ways to explain the unexplainable and their judgement gets clouded. I read a newspaper report that said most people who believed Covid conspiracy theories have degrees and are university educated, so they're not stupid people. They just get obsessed by an idea.

Personally, I think there may have been human error involved in the pandemic and it wouldn't surprise me if, in time, we find out that it did get released from a laboratory, maybe by accident or negligence. But we won't discover the full facts for decades.

The world has experienced a collective wave of negative emotions – fear, frustration, anger. All these things are bad for spirit energy. They create doubt and people become closed off. The good news, however, is that these negative aspects of the pandemic are short-lived and are far outweighed by the good that the world has experienced. All the love, compassion and kindness we've seen has created an awareness of how good it feels to be kind and to love each other. These are just the kind of qualities that nourish spirit energy, as you'll discover later. People's spirituality has been awoken. Many of us have rebalanced our lives and re-evaluated what is important to us.

One of my friends, Jackie, was on the brink of divorce before the pandemic. She had two young children of school age and worked full time in the events industry. They were looked after by a childminder after school and she got home just in time to put them to bed. Her husband, let's call him Jake, worked in the city, put in long hours and earned a good wage. He hardly saw his wife or kids during the week and would often do a few hours of work during the weekend. Even when they were together, they were not present because they were so preoccupied with work and the stresses of everyday life. Therefore, they just drifted apart. There was nothing inherently wrong with their relationship. No one had an affair. They just stopped being together and assumed that was the way life progressed. In a warped way they equated material and financial stability with success. But spiritually they were both withering away.

Jackie confided in me that she was thinking of leaving her husband because they were more like friends than a couple. She felt something missing and when she thought about the future, she could only see the situation getting worse. Jake, a typical man, did his best to ignore things but deep down knew there was a fundamental problem with his marriage.

Then the pandemic hit. Jackie was furloughed, the kids' school was closed as was Jake's office. He was ordered to work from home. They were lucky enough to have space in their house for a home office and also had a garden (I think all those families who lived through lockdown and home-schooled in flats were heroes). Jake and Jackie found themselves suddenly thrown together as a family unit for the first time in many years, with time on their hands. And at first it was tough. They were worried about their jobs and dreaded the idea of having to become teachers to their kids – who incidentally loved the idea of not being in school. They had to pull together, work as a team, live as a family again and learn to enjoy the simple things in life like walks, games and baking. In this they were the same as practically every other household in the country.

I spoke to Jackie around week three of the first lockdown.

"I miss Prosecco lunches," she sighed.

"Don't we all, love," I laughed.

"But you know the good thing, Sally," she said, "me and Jake are getting on really well, better than we've done for years. I forgot what a good father he is."

Today they are solid as a rock and happier than they've been for years. Jackie is still working but has reduced her hours. Jake realised he was unhappy at work and could live without three holidays a year and an apartment in Portugal and is now retraining as a teacher. He had an epiphany; the pandemic shook him out of a stupor.

I'm willing to bet there are a lot of stories like this. People have discovered their souls again, and reconnected with the things that are most important, the things like kindness and love that fuel the spirit.

The pandemic scared everyone. It scared everyone into looking at how fragile we are. There's absolutely no doubt about it. When you face death, either as an individual or as a species, and survive it, something profound happens. Mortality smashes you in the forehead and, if you are lucky, it wakes you up.

Chapter 2

The power in us all

Everyone wants to live a more spiritual life don't they? Being spiritual is good isn't it? But what does being spiritual actually mean?

Some people will describe themselves as spiritual without understanding what it is to be spiritual. We all know that person who spouts off profound platitudes about living a life of positivity and pure thought, while underneath they are negative and self-absorbed. Or the gap-year students who go to some far-flung corner of the world, buy some tie-dye yoga pants and 'find themselves'. While I'm not knocking it, because it is a start, I'm duty-bound to inform these people that a few fridge magnets with inspirational quotes, some wind chimes in the garden and a dream catcher in the bedroom does not make you spiritual.

Of course, if these accessories help people concentrate their awareness on positive thoughts and emotions, that is a good thing. They are tools that can enable people to connect to their spirit energy by providing a focus. But just owning something that relates to spirituality in some way doesn't make you spiritual and it will not help you get in touch with your core spirit power. This book is the exception, obvs, because it provides tangible guidance and also states an immutable truth, which is that you have to do the work to get the rewards.

I used to know a woman who filled her home with pictures of angels and framed inspirational quotes. Her Facebook timeline was full of uplifting posts and she would go on about high vibrational energy and how she would never allow anyone into her life who brought low vibrational energy. She truly believed she was on a higher spiritual plane and was a force for love and positivity in the world. But behind closed doors she'd have regular arguments with her long-suffering partner that showed a real darkness at her core. She'd scream blue murder and bully the poor chap. Under the surface, she was actually a deeply unhappy, bitter and lonely person. She knew this of course, and rather than accept her failings and work on them to make herself a better human, she hid it all behind the mask of spirituality that she presented to the world. This is one of the lessons you learn about spirit early on. It's very easy to spot a fake.

It's no good wishing yourself into a more spiritual existence: that's not going to achieve anything. You can talk the talk all you like, but in order to really connect to your spirit energy you have to walk the walk and live life according to a certain set of values and behaviours, which I will come to in due course – apologies for the delayed gratification!

But first let's explore a little bit about spirituality, what it is and what it is not. The first thing you need to know, is that it's not religion. Spirituality and religion are two very different things as far as I'm concerned.

Religion is a faith system built around a story that people put their belief in. In a way, and in my humble opinion, religion is a sort of cult. I don't mean that in a derogatory sense, but it is an organised institution that provides followers with a set of rules under which they are expected to live, usually in exchange for some form of reward further down the line, usually after death.

Most religions are hierarchical, in that there is usually a body of elevated people tasked with propagating and promoting the ideas and ideals of the religion. On the whole, religion is benevolent and most religions encourage the worship of a higher power, or deity. The message they give to followers is usually if you want to know God, if you want to feel God, then you've got to follow our rules.

It might surprise you to know, given that some religions have traditionally frowned upon people like me and in the old days would drown us in duck ponds, that I think religion is very much needed, because for some people religions provide a form of deep comfort, they give hope and also set out a moral code under which to live.

Spirituality, on the other hand, is more like a mindset. It does have a certain code of ethics, many of which are also shared by religions, and it requires certain behaviours of its adherents, but it does not promise eternal reward in exchange for devotion. It also doesn't come with a set of stories, and it's not promoted by any organisation. It is a state of mind, a way of being. You can be spiritual without being religious although some people need religion to be spiritual in the same way some people can only lose weight if they go to Weight Watchers because they need the rules, structure and a motivating force that an organising body provides.

Lots of people will describe themselves as spiritual without being religious, which makes sense when you consider the two as separate and different. Spirituality is a primal state of being, it is within you and something you *are*, not something that has been created.

The power in us all

The difference between spirituality and religion can be illustrated by considering some people who were either religious or spiritual, but not both. Rasputin was religious, but not spiritual, Osama bin Laden was religious but not spiritual. Meanwhile, on a lighter note, Russell Brand is spiritual but not religious, as is Gwyneth Paltrow.

Mixed in with the idea of spirituality, which is something we can all access and practise, is the concept of spirit. There are lots of different interpretations of what a spirit is. Some say it's your soul, your lifeforce or your essence. Some describe ghosts as spirits. Both are correct in my opinion.

To me, your spirit sits at the core of your existence and powers you. It's the part of you made from a pure type of energy – spirit energy. This is like a battery and exists on two planes, or dimensions. It exists as an integral part of your physical body, but also lives in the world beyond the one we experience in our conscious-ness – the Earth plane – a world which I call the 'spirit plane'. I know this is a fairly out-there concept to grapple with, but it helps to visualise your spirit as a glowing ball of energy (like electricity but not as dangerous) sitting in the centre of your chest, gently shimmering in time with your breath. If you focus your concentration on your chest and imagine that glowing ball, you can sometimes feel it sitting there. It is a living thing: in fact it's your life. It contains all your memories and the love you receive and give others.

Spirit energy is made of love and you can feed it by striving to be good to yourself and to others. The more love you give and receive, and the more good deeds you do in life, the more powerful your energy will be. The stronger your energy, the more connections it can make to the spirit world. Powerful spirit energy attracts other spirit energy. It is magnetic and spirit energy isn't self-contained within you. It sends out millions of tiny filaments that connect with all the other energy around it, both here on Earth plane and in the spirit plane. It's like an immense spiderweb of connections that constantly shift and change and link up. As we move through life, our energy flows from us and around us. The universe beyond observable matter is made of this energy. It is the building block of everything metaphysical and it is what is left when the physical matter we are made of is destroyed. It's the unifying, permanent force that links everything together.

If this all sounds a bit *Star Wars*, that's because it is. In the famous movies there is a unifying energy called the Force which has a dark side and a light side and which connects all living things. It's what Luke Skywalker uses to defeat Darth Vader. Quite amazingly, George Lucas, the movie's director, was on to something when he wrote the films. I wouldn't be surprised if he was a medium too, because he seems to know a lot about the underlying power that controls the universe. The only difference is that I like to call this guiding power 'spirit energy' rather than the Force, and it is not occurring a long time ago in a galaxy far, far away, it's happening here and now and doesn't just affect aliens, it affects you, your Auntie Beryl and everyone around you. And you don't have to be a Jedi Knight to benefit from it or control it.

Not only can you harness this energy, you can also feed it and increase it, and that's the practice of spirituality, which is about being aware of the capability within you and being able to trust and listen to it. I'll be describing more about this later in this book. Think of me as Yoda, training you to use spirit energy. And while you might not be able to destroy a Death Star after your training, you will be connected to the energy of the universe in a more meaningful way.

*   *   *

The important thing to understand is that spirit energy is accessible to all of us. You don't need special powers. We can all feel it and tap into it. The difference with mediums is that we can connect with it and decipher the information that it holds.

I came to this conclusion because of the way the process works when I am on stage. I realised that one of the keys to harnessing this power was that all the people in the audience shared the same openness to the possibilities of spirit. This is important, because an openness and acceptance of spirit allows energy to flow between people unimpeded.

This is one of the key lessons behind the spirit secret. Openness is everything. The reason, I believe, is to do with some kind of structure inside us all that acts like a valve. I've no idea what form it takes. It might be a psychological thing, like a state of mind, or it might even be a tiny structure in our brains or even a chemical, that works to unlock the part of our minds which open to spirit and allow the energy in us to connect with the energy around us. Whatever it is, we all have this structure or ability, it's a part of the human body, just like a heart or a lung or the ability to think. When you are born, it is open, which explains why children are so much more in tune with otherworldly things, why they see and hear things that adults can't.

I also think this applies to animals. They also share this biological or psychological quirk and can connect with spirit energy. This explains why dogs and cats frequently react to things we don't sense. When you are born, this valve is open and allows spirit energy to flow through you but as we grow it starts to close. As children, when we react to things that adults don't perceive, we are told to stop being so silly, so we learn to hide our powers and over time as the valve gets used less and less it becomes weak. Modern life doesn't allow us to use this function as much as we would have done thousands of years ago. Today there are distractions everywhere. We are busy, we are glued to our mobile phones and social media and we rarely have the opportunity to listen to our bodies and minds and to follow our natural intuitiveness, which is what this structure facilitates. All this interference affects both out spiritual lives and our brains and takes us further away from the wonders of spirit.

We can reclaim our spiritual heritage, however. I noticed that the more I was exposed to high levels of spirit energy during my live shows, the more developed my ability to connect with spirit seemed to get. Which suggested to me that using this valve was like exercising a muscle.

The thing about this theory is that not so long ago the realm of science would have labelled it preposterous. Science and psychics don't generally mix. But then, a couple of years ago I had a visit from a scientist who was so fascinated with what I did he had decided to book for a reading. When he arrived he seemed more interested in what I was doing and the process I was using than the messages he was getting from the reading, which I thought was odd. He was honest from the beginning and told me he was a scientist and that he was studying my work. I wasn't too surprised, because many years before that I had been involved in an experiment when another scientist came along and tested my remote reading skills. I passed with flying colours and the man wrote about his experiences in a newspaper story.

This chap was short, in his fifties , clean shaven and serious. He wore jeans and a t-shirt and carried a leather attaché case. He spoke in a soft Welsh accent and had a deep voice.

I sat him down in front of me, made a bit of small talk to get him comfortable and he got a pad out of his bag, put it on his lap and asked if I minded him taking notes.

"Of course not, love," I said.

I took a breath and closed my eyes briefly, which is what I do sometimes as a way to clear my mind and open myself up to spirit.

I heard his pen scratch the paper and glanced down momentarily at his pad.

"Breath. Closed eyes," he'd written.

"Strange," I thought.

"I'm getting mixed feelings. I can feel that you are quite sceptical, and that's fine," I told him (I've been tested several times in the past, so it doesn't faze me when someone turns up with an ulterior motive).

He was very calm.

"I'm here because I'm interested in what you do," he said. "Please proceed."

I focused my mind and concentrated on the energy that was around him. I could feel the presence of a woman closely connected to him and when I concentrated, I could see her face in my mind's eye. She looked tired and drawn, she was very pale. Her age was hard to place, but she wasn't old, she just looked old. I knew she was his mother and she had been ill.

"Your mother is in spirit," I said. "I have her here. She looks very tired."

He didn't say anything, but he shifted in his chair. His expression changed slightly, from dispassionate to surprised. He indicated for me to continue.

The lady in spirit was showing me a scene. She was in bed in a bright sunny room. There were flowers in a vase on a bedside table, and the place felt comfortable but slightly clinical.

"She was in a hospice," I said.

Next to the flowers on the nightstand there was a family photo. The woman was in it, along with a man I realised was her husband and two older teenagers, a boy and a girl. They were all smiling. I recognised the boy in the photo as the man sitting in front of me.

I smiled.

"She had a photo of you all together by her bedside," I said.

He nodded. He'd been scribbling notes but stopped.

"Yes, she did," he said softly.

What happened next has happened to me a thousand times. When I am giving readings to people who are reticent or sceptical it often takes a key piece of information to unlock them, like turning a key. Once that lock is open, the true meaning of that message comes tumbling out. I can almost feel the connection as the barrier breaks down and the person in spirit and the person with me connect properly.

I felt the intensity of the love between mother and son.

The scene that I was feeling became more focused. She was in the same bed but barely conscious. Her husband and daughter were either side of her, holding her hand and crying. I described this to the man with me. I understood the significance of what she was showing me and what she needed me to tell her son.

"She's showing me the end. You weren't there," I said. The man had tears in his eyes now and I could sense his sorrow.

"She says that it doesn't matter. She wasn't alone and she understands why you couldn't get there in time. You need to let go of the guilt. She loves you so much and she doesn't want you to be sad."

By this time the poor bloke was in pieces. Tears were dripping onto his pad.

I pulled a tissue from the box I kept on the table in my office for such occasions and handed it to him.

"It can be quite an emotional experience," I said to him as he took a moment to compose himself.

We chatted about his mother, who he explained had died of cancer several years before when he was studying at Cambridge and doing his PhD.

"It's unusual for someone from the scientific community to go to a psychic," I questioned.

"I think there is truth in the strangest of places," he said to me cryptically.

He then started to question me about how I did what I did and what I believed was behind it all. I explained my belief about spirit energy. He said he believed I was on to something and then explained that he worked in the field of quantum mechanics and was a quantum physicist. I had no idea what that meant or what he did in his day-to-day job, but he explained to me on a very basic level that quantum physics is concerned with the world of matter in its smallest form, below atoms. At this scale, he explained, reality is very weird. The building blocks of matter are not just particles, they are also waves and fields of energy and everything connects. Things can exist in two places at the same time and time itself means something different.

To be honest, he lost me after about 10 minutes, but he was very excited about what he'd witnessed.

As we chatted, I explained that messages build in intensity and appeared to be attracted to other messages as though there is some form of magnetism drawing them together in clumps. I said that I believed the energy is life essence and is one of the fundamental ingredients of the universe, not just the universe we inhabit but the universe of the afterlife as well. It is the one constant force that bridges across the realm of the living and the realm of the dead and which makes us what we are.

"Who knows, maybe one day we will be able to put it under a microscope and study it," I shrugged.

He laughed. "More like a particle accelerator," he said.

I didn't have a clue what he was talking about.

He asked me how I thought energy worked and I explained that since I had started touring, I had learned how to harness it and make it work in an environment where there were lots of people and lots of messages all coming through at the same time. "I think it wants to connect to the energy all around," I said. "It works best when you accept it and open yourself to it, when you allow it to flow freely. It connects to something inside your body."

He was fascinated by what I felt when I was connected to other people's energy and how I received the messages and information that formed the basis of the reading I'd just given him. I explained that I cleared my mind and just allowed it to come in, that it wasn't conscious thought, but images, ideas and information that seemed to be placed in my mind, or that flowed through it. I said that sometimes the connection can be so strong that I take on aspects of the personality of the spirit that the energy is from: their gait, their vocabulary, how they felt at the ends of their lives. It is quite incredible and fascinating.

"It's like electricity in a wall socket," I said. "We can't see it but if you took the cover off the socket and put your finger in it, you'd feel it."

All the while he took notes, raising an eyebrow now and then.

"Do you have to believe in the process?" he asked.

"I think it helps when you trust in the process," I answered. "You can be sceptical and question what's happening, but I think when you trust that what you are experiencing is a real thing, then you can feel it and focus on it better."

I thought about how the process worked during live shows. How I would usually start to feel energy connections in the hours before I went on stage and how as the audience started to fill up the auditorium, I would start to hear and see things in my mind's eye in the form of flashes of images: faces, scenes, places and objects. Then the voices would start. I'd hear places, names of loved ones. Sometimes I'd get glimpses of scenes. I can only imagine that anyone who had experienced anything similar without understanding what was happening to them, even on a small scale, would be terrified and would reach the conclusion that they were experiencing some form of mental health emergency.

I'd noticed over the years that there seemed to be a kind of attraction that drew energy together and often resulted in messages with a similar theme. I recalled one of the hundreds of shows I've hosted. It was a freezing night at a theatre in the north of England and I remembered standing in the wings, waiting to go on, surrounded by an aura of energy through which I could sense individual spirits. If I'd had some kind of magical psychic X-ray specs, I would have been able to see arcs of energy criss-crossing from the stage to the seats as connections were made between those in spirit and those in the audience. Those arcs would have varied in thickness; some would be as thick as rope, others would be just a faint trace of light. It was an ever-changing network of connections.

I had been touring for five years at that point and was beginning to gain a real understanding of how the process worked. I knew that everything was driven by this invisible energy and that somehow patterns formed during each show. I would give a message to someone in the audience and by doing that I would create an energy connection to them. This would draw in other messages. Spirits were attracted to areas of the audience where connections had already been made.

That evening started with a very specific message which made a strong energy connection. I could sense the energy of a man in spirit standing next to me. I sensed his name was Andy and I could hear words in my mind. When I say "hear", I don't mean sounds. That's not how it works. The information appears as thoughts, but they are not *my* thoughts. They drop into my subconscious along with images and other detail and I go along with them and what they are telling me. That is where the trust element comes in. After all this time I trust that those feelings and the intuition they give me mean something to someone. I'm feeling them for a reason.

In this instance Andy, or rather his energy, led me across the stage to an area of the audience midway up in the stalls and directed me to a group of women.

"I have a lovely man here called Andy," I explained. Other details dropped into my mind. I saw the number 55 and the names Debbie, Carole and Angela. As this was happening in my head, I described it exactly to the audience, again trusting that it would mean something to someone.

It is not always an exact art and sometimes the details come through jumbled. This, I believe, is because there are sometimes lots of connections linking different energies.

But as soon as I said the names I was being given, I heard a gasp from the audience and saw a hand go up. In the same way I felt the connection between the scientist and his mother, I felt the connection being made between Andy in spirit and the woman in the audience who raised her hand. It felt like a surge of electricity going through me.

The woman stood and explained that her name was Carole, she was with one of her sisters, Debbie, and had another sister, Angela. Her father, Andy, had died three years ago aged 55.

Of the hundreds of readings I've done in shows over the years this one always sticks out because of the instant accuracy. And it got even more freaky.

I began the process of linking the living with their loved ones in spirit. Andy talked to them through me. He gave me information specific to his death and told me how his daughters were around his bedside when he passed.

"He thanks you for that," I told the women. "You made it much easier for him."

And then I started to feel hot, and I could smell smoke. Often the information from spirit energy comes in the form of different stimuli, such as sense, touch, taste and smell. I described all this to them, and Carole said that her father had been a firefighter.

I felt an uncomfortable burning sensation and started to smell an altogether more unpleasant smell, like burning flesh.

"Oh my God," I gasped. "Did he get burnt in an accident?"

Carole and Debbie looked blankly at each other and shook their heads. Andy had never been injured in the line of duty.

"But someone burned in a fire," I said. By this stage I was concentrating so hard on what I was feeling and experiencing in my mind that I wasn't immediately aware of the person a few seats to the left of the sisters who was waving a hand.

Then I heard another name in my mind.

"And who is Mel or Melissa?" I asked.

The sisters continued to shake their heads.

Finally, I noticed the hand waving and when I said hello to the woman it belonged to, I knew intuitively that this was another message for her, and that Andy's energy had drawn in the energy from another spirit.

I asked the woman to stand so I could see her more clearly. I had learned from experience that the clearer the connection between me and the person whose message I was channelling, the clearer the message tended to be. The theory worked both in physical connection, face-to-face, and also through a screen.

As I said hello to the woman in the audience, I felt the presence of a woman by the side of me. In my mind I could see an image of her and it was horrific. She was badly burned down the left side of her face. Her skin was hanging in charred strips from her face and neck.

I wish I could say that over the years, having been exposed to such images on countless occasions, I'd got used to the blood and gore and broken bodies that spirits like to show me. I honestly think sometimes they do it to see how I react. After all, they can be mischievous. Other times they do it because it represents their last moments on the Earth plane. No matter how many times I see these types of shocking images they still make me jump.

I gently told the lady in the audience what I was seeing, sparing her from the finer details, and asked if she had a female relative in spirit who died in a fire.

She confirmed that she had. Her aunt Melissa had died because of a house fire. A theme was beginning to build around that specific area of the audience. Melissa's energy had been attracted to Andy's energy, because he was a fireman. That was the link. From there the links continued. I discovered that Melissa had been a twin but her twin sister had died in childbirth. As I was explaining that I was picking this information up, and having it confirmed to me by Melissa's niece, I also started to feel the presence of another set of male twins in spirit, one of whom was directing me towards another section of the audience and to a woman whose dead father was a twin.

To begin with, when I started touring, these links had appeared irregularly and haphazardly. But increasingly over the years they had become more pronounced. I was fascinated by the way it worked, and how it all seemed to be connected and I came up with a name for the process. I called it *message building*.

I explained all this to the scientist, who we'll call Igor, not because that was his name, but because it's a funny name for a scientist. I'm sure he wouldn't want me to give away his real name or identify him, because even though he agreed that something scientific was happening and he was fascinated by the idea of energy, because it seemed to share many of the properties he was studying in quantum physics, I would imagine his peers would laugh him out of the lab if they knew he'd been to see a psychic.

However, if there's one lesson we could all take to heart from his open-mindedness, it's that we should always be open to possibility. If we always think the same way and do the same things, we never discover anything new. This applies to so many areas of life, from the places we go on holiday to scientific research. Life should be about seeking out new things and taking risks, not staying in the same old patterns doing the same old things.

Igor was eager to know what I thought happened to our energy when we died and how it is connected to the wider universe. I explained that in a natural, old-age death, I believed that the body, which is an organic vessel, ceases to function because it is no longer needed and that the energy then converts into its pure state. The process was different for sudden death, but the result was still the same. The energy survives outside the body. It's not destroyed. We then got into a deep philosophical conversation that made my brain ache.

"Why do you think the body dies though? Why don't we live forever if energy is infinite?" Igor pushed.

"Erm, maybe we are here for a purpose and when we've served that purpose our energy moves on," I said.

"Where does it go?" he asked.

"I've always thought of the afterlife as another dimension. Somewhere that exists alongside the space we live in and experience. Energy can cross between the two."

He was really making me think.

"Where does the energy come from?"

This was a biggie. The more I think about it, the more I believe that energy is part of the fabric of the universe and has been here forever and little bits of it break off and form clumps that inhabit us and give us our souls.

"Energy can neither be destroyed or created," explained Igor. "It exists. Is this what you are saying?"

"I suppose so," I answered.

And this led to one of the most perplexing questions of my work and of spirit power: what's the point of it all?

I don't mean that in a frivolous way, but we all wonder at some point in our lives, why are we here? What's the grand plan? One school of thought supposes that it's a lucky fluke. Chemicals and energy managed to combine eons ago to create an organic molecule that evolved into the human species and will continue to evolve to become something else if we don't manage to make ourselves extinct first. But I'm not so sure. When you start to peel back the curtain, and see the complexities of spirit energy, and how it exists on different planes, you realise that there must be a plan, or that some guiding hand is behind this.

Religions will point to God or gods, in all his/her/their/its forms (what pronoun do you use for a divine force?). I'm not religious and I don't believe in the traditional idea of God: old man, beard, flowing robes, anger issues, woke son.

I do, however, believe in divinity, which is a higher power that guides the ebb and flow of our reality. I think we all submit to divinity in our own ways because it's written in our psyche, this need to honour someone or something. We all have a need to believe in and strive for something better or bigger or more divine than that which we are. It can be a purpose, or a state of being. I think we all know deep down that there is something there, beyond us and better than us, and that death brings us closer to it. Why, when anyone talks about death, do they habitually look up to the sky, even when they don't believe the idea of heaven in the clouds? It's because we know there is something beyond this life, something else out there.

It is a miracle that we are made the way we are and it follows a logical line that there's been some form of intervention to get us to be so. I can't believe that we are random chemical and biological quirks in a single chaotic universe, particularly not when I experience what I do when I connect with the spirit realm.

I'm not a scientist like Igor and I haven't studied quantum physics. My theories are all hypothetical, of course, but they are based on decades of observations and experiences that can only be explained by the existence of spirit energy.

Igor and I talked at length about my theories and he took everything I said deadly seriously. He didn't scoff and he was hungry for knowledge.

"I don't think you are a million miles away from the truth," he said.

He explained to me that in quantum physics there are two types of particles: matter (or stuff you can touch) and force (energy), and that the two connect in ways we barely understand. Everything we do connects to the rest of the universe in some infinitesimal way. Every action creates tiny ripples through the fabric of the universe that radiate out to the end of space and time. That's quite a concept to get your head around. In my opinion that's how energy works. We exist in a field of it, moving through it and beyond it.

"I really believe you are on the right track," he said. And then he started explaining about time, and how it can be jumbled and folded. He lost me completely.

When he left, he thanked me for sharing my thoughts with him and after that I never saw or heard from him again. I still don't know if I was part of a bigger experiment and if he ever wrote a theory about what he experienced. I was just glad I could pass on the message from his mum. I got the impression it made a real impact on him and helped him find peace with an event in his past that had obviously been troubling him for some years.

And I think that's the point of spirit energy. It presents itself for a reason and that reason is inherently good. This in turn is why I think there is some divine design to all of this. I was given the ability to read energy and connect with it for a reason. It wasn't random. When I conduct readings, I say I am talking to the dead because that's a snappy headline. It is easy to understand. But in reality, what I am really doing is linking to the energy previously connected to those who have crossed to another dimension and taking the information that that specific clump of energy holds. It is a living thing. It contains a conscience, and each node contains the personality of the individual it was, but they are also part of a much bigger reality, like billions of stars in the universe.

I don't read science books or journals but I do read and watch the news and I know scientists are developing incredible machines to try to uncover the mysteries of quantum physics and the universe. Experiments like the Large Hadron Collider are discovering evidence of particles smaller than atoms – they call one of them the God Particle. Soon we'll have quantum computers more powerful than anything we can imagine, on which scientists can run artificial intelligence programmes that will discover further mysteries and solve some of the planet's biggest problems. The cure for cancer, the solution to clean energy and climate change, these things are tantalisingly close. It is not beyond the realms of possibility to imagine that in a few short decades, science will have saved us and uncovered some of the biggest questions about our existence that have been puzzling mankind for generations. And when it does, I wonder whether somewhere, a scientist called 'Igor' will be smiling wryly and saying to himself, "I'll be damned. She was right."

Chapter 3

Afterlife

Firstly, some general housekeeping.

The world of spirit comes with its own vocabulary and different phrases might mean different things depending on who you are talking to. Some people, for example, will take 'ghost', 'soul' and 'spirit' to mean the same thing. There is a subtle difference, however. I use spirit to describe the energy that I've spoken about in the previous chapters. It manifests itself as a general force, or, in readings and mediumship, as an individual entity representative of the person that it previously embodied. Souls are our non-physical beings. They are the part of us made of energy which carry our memories and personalities and live on when our physical bodies die. Ghosts, on the other hand, are also spirit, but they are visual representations.

Then we have things such as orbs, which are tiny dots of light. These are also physical manifestations of spirit at a very early stage. They are spirits saying, I want to be seen. They usually indicate that there is a growing intensity of energy, and they can build into a more visual expression of energy, maybe a mist, or smoke. Sometimes they augur an expression based around a different sense, like sound or smell.

For many years I lived in an old rectory in Surrey which was haunted by the spirit of one of the former vicars. Often my husband, John, and I would be sitting in the lounge watching TV and an orb would make its way across the room followed by a strong smell of incense. That was the vicar making his presence known to us.

Ghost images used to be seldom captured, because people didn't carry cameras around with them all the time and rarely filmed themselves before the days of mobile phones and social media. Nowadays we all have cameras in our pockets and in an increasingly social media-obsessed world, everyone is filming themselves. This has led to an upswing in ghost images, some of which are genuine, some of which can be explained by tricks of the light.

In recent years I've been lucky enough to capture the fairly clear images of two ghosts, one of which was the vicar, which I have on film and which caused quite a stir when it made headlines in the newspapers.

It happened as I was filming something for one of my social media channels and felt something behind me. Then out of the corner of my eye I saw him zoom past me, close to my shoulder. He then rose through the ceiling in front of me. You can see me shriek on the footage.

Another time I was filming one of my regular social media shows on my table, which I had specially made in Finland. It's made of ancient wood and has weird runes carved in it. In the footage you can clearly see a ghostly skull floating above the table, reflected in the varnish.

These are representations of different sorts of ghosts, and I think ghosts vary because of the energy, not necessarily of the spirit, but of the receiver – that is, the person who sees them. And also because of the environment in which they appear, which explains why older buildings are more likely to be haunted. They contain more energy, which fills them like a residue.

I believe this because many years ago I saw a ghost when I was staying with friends in America and it appeared as solid as a real, living person. It was so realistic I thought it was a living person.

Our friends lived in a beautiful old house in Westport, Connecticut, and we used to visit them every year. The house was formerly a children's home where troubled and wayward teenagers from New York and Boston went for holidays and therapy. Over the years so many children had passed through it that they had left imprints of their energies.

One evening, I retired to my room and decided to settle down and watch a *Harry Potter* DVD. I'd never seen any of the films and it was the only DVD in the room. I settled down in bed and got engrossed in the adventures of Harry, Hermione and Ron. The friends I was staying with had a daughter, Charlotte, who is grown up and married now, but at the time she was 11. About 30 minutes into the movie, I felt her next to me and saw her face up against mine.

She made me jump and I exclaimed, "Oh, Charlotte, you frightened me." I glanced at her and she smiled slightly and moved away. I looked back at the screen and idly discussed the film. She was silent and then seemed to glide to the back and out of the room. As she was a gymnast and a dancer, I assumed she was doing a moonwalk and commended her on the move. The door then opened and she left.

The next morning, I was in the kitchen with my friend Di, Charlotte's mum, making a cup of tea and Charlotte came in.

"You could have stayed and watched the movie with me last night," I said. "But I was impressed with the moonwalking."

She looked at me and frowned.

"What are you talking about?"

"When you came in my room," I explained.

"I didn't," she laughed.

Di gasped.

"On my God Sally," she said. "You saw Lucky."

She explained that the family had all seen her, even her husband, Jim, who was a complete sceptic. He was a city trader and had been working late one night when he heard footsteps running down the hall, which he assumed belonged to Charlotte. He caught sight of what he thought was his daughter out of the corner of his eye and was surprised to see her wearing a skirt printed with poodles. He called out to her and told her to get back to bed and to take off her mother's skirt. The following morning, he told his wife and asked her if she had a dog print skirt that she'd loaned to Charlotte. She didn't, and Charlotte had been asleep in her room all night. That was the first time Lucky appeared to the family.

Di explained to me that Lucky resided in the loft room and later I connected with her spirit again and I learned that she had lived in the attic and had committed suicide by jumping from the window there. I'm not sure why she was called Lucky, given the information, but her ghost was so pronounced because of the energy in the property, and she was mischievous in spirit because she had been mischievous in life.

Every example of a ghost appearing – also sometimes called an apparition – is unique to the circumstances. For example, when I caught the vicar on video, I had been doing a video reading for a woman whose name was Sally Anne. The vicar appeared the moment I said the name Sally. I think he wanted to come and tell me that he didn't want me to do readings for other people in the room I was in, because it was his room.

There is a long rich history of ghosts and hauntings in the UK. The case of the Enfield Poltergeist is one of the most famous. Over 18 months starting from the summer of 1977, 284 Green Street in Enfield, North London became the site of a well-documented poltergeist haunting. The tenant, Peggy Hodgson, her children and over 30 eyewitnesses, including neighbours, psychic researchers, journalists and even the local lollipop lady, saw and heard moving furniture, flying objects, unexplained knocking noises and levitation.

The activity was centred on the daughters, Janet and Margaret, with 11-year-old Janet acting as the conduit for a mysterious, gruff voice which identified itself as a former resident of the house, Bill Wilkins, who died at the age of 72. He was cross-examined by Richard Grosse, the son of psychic investigator Maurice Grosse. As a newly qualified solicitor, Richard helped his father interrogate the Enfield poltergeist and, as such, is probably the only member of the Law Society to have cross-examined a ghost. He asked Bill if he remembered how he died. Bill replied, via Janet's voice, "I had a haemorrhage, and I fell asleep, and I died in a chair, in the corner downstairs." The voice also announced, "I'm invisible... because I'm a G.H.O.S.T." The story – of dying in a corner seat in the living room – was later corroborated by Mr Wilkins' son.

Janet and Margaret were interviewed many years later and stuck by their stories. Janet summed it up by saying, "I was used and abused – there was levitation, there was the voices and then there was... the curtain that wrapped itself around my neck, which was quite life-threatening for me, and it brought it home to me – that this could kill you." Many people thought the family invented it all, using basic conjuring tricks, in order to get a new and better council house.

The events were used as a template for another famous spooky case, the BBC's famous spoof ghost hunt,

Ghostwatch, which was broadcast on Halloween night in 1992, and was watched by 11 million people.

The supposedly 'live' investigation into paranormal activity was broadcast from a family home in Northolt, north-west London. Michael Parkinson, one of the BBC's most trusted faces, presented it alongside children's television presenter Sarah Greene and her husband, Mike Smith.

The broadcast used infra-red, heat-seeking cameras to film ghostly activity in 'the most haunted house in Britain', where Pamela Early and her two daughters were said to be spooked by a poltergeist. Viewers were told a team of researchers had spent the last 10 months investigating the mysterious movements of a ghost named Pipes – so-called because it kept banging on the water pipes.

As Sarah followed the paranormal activity around the house, the tension mounted, and the Early family were subjected to increasingly terrifying experiences as the spirit of a dead man apparently possessed the children. By the end of the show the ghost had possessed the cameras; paramedics and police were seen arriving at the house and Sarah, who was trying to locate one of the possessed girls, disappeared into the blackness.

Back in the studio, havoc broke out, lights exploded, the crew fled and eventually the floor was deserted apart from a dumbfounded Parky who began to read spooky lines from an autocue which was apparently under the spell of the ghost.

The producers had failed to judge the reaction to the programme, however. Many child viewers were left traumatised, and others complained that the corporation had treated them like mugs by duping them. Tragically, five days after the programme, one 18-year-old viewer, Martin Denham, who had been increasingly agitated by the programme, took his own life. The radiators in the Denham family house had a habit of being noisy when warming up and Martin asked to move bedrooms after the show and seemed fixated with the talk of ghosts, according to his parents. A suicide note to his mum read, "If there is ghosts I will now be one and I will always be with you as one."

* * *

Ghosts can be problematic for people. Although they usually mean no harm, it is quite disconcerting to encounter them, because invariably they appear when you are not expecting them. Even someone like me, well versed in such things, gets freaked out by apparitions. I'm fortunate enough never to have encountered a malevolent ghost or a poltergeist.

Often, people who discover they live in a property and share it with a ghost want to get rid of their other-worldly cohabitor. I can understand why people would, because it's scary, because you're seeing something that shouldn't be there, therefore you're frightened. But I think they have as much right to be there as you do. In fact, that's one of the reasons why they come back to specific locations. The vicar lived in the rectory before I did. It was his home. When people have said to me, "I think I've got a ghost in my house, I don't know if I like it. Could you come and have a look?" I say no, because the spirits definitely know that I am a medium and when they realise that I can see them, they tend to increase activity. It would be like poking a hornet's nest. If you have a ghost in your house that isn't malevolent and no one's being possessed, it's best to learn to live with it.

This is, perhaps, a good time to mention another aspect of spirit: demons. They do exist but are, thankfully, very rare.

Spirit energy is inherently good but sometimes it can be bad. The world of spirit and the dimension spirits reside in is balanced, just like our world is, and so with good sometimes comes bad, as is the way here. There are dark and evil aspects. Like attracts like when it comes to energy, so good attracts good and bad attracts bad. In the same way that you can generate your own good energy and unlock your hidden power, you can also create bad energy or find yourself in a situation where there is bad energy around you.

Unfortunately, some people will move into a property where there is bad energy, or they'll be connected to something, or pick up something that has bad energy. In these situations, I would strongly recommend taking measures to try to get rid of that energy. I've never allowed my work to be part of that element of spirit and so I'm not able and expert in removing bad energy. Quite honestly, the fact that I am so scared of it and really don't want anything to do with it tells me that I shouldn't become involved, which is why when I've been asked to perform exorcisms, I've politely declined.

* * *

Another way of thinking about all of this is that ghost visitations and orbs are two of the methods spirits use to communicate with us. This can be through mediums, but there's not always a medium handy when a spirit wants to make itself known, so a further way they can communicate is by showing us a sign, which is more subtle than appearing as a ghost.

Afterlife

Spirits know what you are thinking and they can decide to let you know they are around, particularly at times when you need them or when they want to show support. A sign can come in many forms, such as a white feather, a butterfly or a robin. It can also be a song on the radio that reminds you of someone. I know that birds lose their feathers all the time, and that songs come on the radio, and obviously not every feather you see or familiar song you hear is a sign from a loved one in the afterlife. The key is timing and context. So, if you're walking down the road, perfectly happy, nothing on your mind apart from what you're having for dinner later and a feather falls in front of you, it is because a bird has flown overhead, or the wind has blown it. If, however, you are stressed or upset about something, or you have recently had bad news or thought about a loved one who has passed that you miss, and then a feather drifts in front of you, that is a sign. That's the difference.

To give an example, I was doing a show at a theatre on the south coast. I'd had a tough week and was recovering from a chest infection. I was tired and to top it off I'd had a few business problems. John and I had been snapping at each other on the phone, as all couples do from time to time, and just before I went on stage I was in my dressing room thinking about my granddad, George. We were very close and although he passed many years ago, I still miss him. He would always be the voice of reason, and the one to help me put things into perspective. He would also cheer me up when I was feeling down. I mouthed a little prayer to him and went on stage. As the applause died down and I welcomed the audience, a white feather floated down in front of me and I felt the familiar presence of my grandfather and a rush of energy sweeping aside my feelings of exhaustion. The spotlight picked it out. Several people in the front row gasped.

"Did you see that?" I asked.

"It was a white feather," a lady answered.

Exhilarated, I called for the house lights to go up and when the stage was fully lit, I started to look around for what I knew was a sign. But it was nowhere to be seen.

It was a sign and presented itself in that form at that moment because it wouldn't have been practical for my granddad to appear as a ghost on the stage when so many other spirits were there, lined up to give messages. He just wanted me to know that I was loved; he didn't want to freak out the audience.

Granddad has form when it comes to appearing as a ghost. He died when I was young and he lived in the house with us up until his death in hospital. We lived in the basement of the house and Mum and Dad had been with him in hospital and they both came home after he died and fell asleep because they'd been up with him all night. Mum woke and felt him there with her. She looked over at the staircase leading down to our flat and saw the outline of a man in smoke. She said it was like someone being revealed, and then he disappeared. He'd only been dead a couple of hours. I think he was desperately trying to show himself. Perhaps it's the case that we have to learn to be in spirit and we take with us our natural instinct to be close to the people we love, in places we are familiar with. Our first instinct would be to go home and to try to work out how to let those who love us know that we are there.

There are ways you can connect with those in spirit that will encourage signs from them. Think about them a lot, keep them in your thoughts, say their name and you will start to notice the signs appearing. My advice is to try to connect with people you know and love and to connect with them for the right reasons, not just to go ghost hunting, because there is a danger you might attract something you can't control.

*   *   *

While ghosts are quite easy to explain, because many people have either seen them (or seen *Ghostbusters*), souls are bit harder to understand because they are not visible and they are more closely aligned with us as individuals. A soul is the essence of a person. It's the aspect of us that lives on after we die, like a vessel into which all the non-corporeal things about us are stored. A soul is what makes us who we are.

If you are puzzled by the concept of a soul, you are not alone. Philosophers, religious leaders and even scientists have attempted to work out what a soul is for thousands of years. In many traditions it's seen as the immortal essence of a person and is without form. In 1907 a doctor in the US named Duncan MacDougall even went as far as trying to weigh a soul. He proposed that the human soul weighed 21 grams. In an experiment he placed six dying patients on beds fitted with sensitive weighing mechanisms and measured them just before and just after they died. In each case he recorded a sudden, unexplained weight loss of 21 grams, which he said was not caused by any natural process. He concluded that the sudden loss could only be explained by the soul leaving the body and that the soul must therefore weigh 21 grams.

He repeated the experiment on dogs but recorded no weight loss at the time of death and so surmised that dogs do not have souls. I know for a fact this is wrong, because I regularly get dogs and all sorts of other animals coming through to me when I do readings. MacDougall's notes were published in an academic journal, but his findings and methods have long been questioned by other academics.

A soul is different from our consciousness, which is equally mysterious. Consciousness is how we experience the world. It is the awareness we have of ourselves, the world around us and our place within it.

Death and souls are intrinsically linked because our souls survive death. To so many people, death seems like the cruellest part of being human. It is something we all experience. Each of us will lose a loved one at some point in our lives and then each of us will in turn die. Of everything we go through in life, death is the one inevitability, which can seem a bit grim at times, because overall most people do not want to die. There are three main reasons for this. Firstly, many see death as a painful process and something that is arrived at after terrible illness, discomfort or an agonising accident. Secondly, most of us enjoy life and have people in our lives who we love. We don't want to leave them and we don't want to stop doing the things we enjoy. And, thirdly, there is the fear of the unknown. It takes trust and faith to realise that there is an afterlife and unfortunately many people are persuaded against a belief that there is another life after death because of sceptical voices.

We can't ignore the fact that some deaths can be painful, but that pain passes as soon as we pass. It is replaced by peace and bliss. There is no pain in the afterlife because pain is something which we experience through our bodies. Souls do not have bones to break or skin to cut. They don't have a nervous system. When we die, we discard our bodies and with them the ability to be hurt. We are set free from the ailments and disabilities that held us back when we lived. Over the years I have received messages from thousands of people in spirit who suffered during life and in every case, there is no hint of pain in the afterlife, only relief and freedom.

There is also no sense of loss in the afterlife because our energy is always linked to our loved ones, living and dead. The love we have for each other when we are alive does not stop when we die. Loss and grief are only suffered by the living.

So why do we die? Well quite simply it is the natural order of things. Dying is part of the process of life: everything on the planet has a lifespan. We are lucky if we live to 100. We have a short lifespan in relation to some organisms and a long one in relation to others. We live on a single planet with limited space and if no one died our part of the physical universe would soon become overcrowded. Life is finite, it has to be. It is the bit afterwards that is infinite. Death is part of the overall plan. Some tragic deaths appear to be unfairly random and against the natural order of things, such as when children die. However, I believe we all die when we are meant to. The same applies to all forms of life.

We are emotional creatures and we love each other and when what we perceive as the natural order of things is upset, when someone dies out of sync, we get upset and angry. We talk of people dying too soon and we question why it happens. Losing children is the wrong way round after all isn't it? Parents should not outlive offspring. But people die. That is the fact of the matter. They get sick and they die, sometimes they don't get sick and they die. And the reason for it is that the energy we hold inside us, that makes us who we are, is not meant to be held on to. It is part of the balance of the wider universe we have yet to fully understand.

Science and medicine have made huge strides in keeping people alive and beating diseases. Undoubtedly this is a good thing. However, I am not always sure that it is right to use science as a way of overcoming death, or at least holding it at bay when death is the natural progression. There are times when people should be allowed to go. It is in our nature to want to keep people alive. We all have a survival instinct and know how precious life is and should most definitely follow that and prevent suffering with medicine if we can. However, most people know when it is their time to go and would want to go with dignity. Quality of life is the most important thing. Being involved in life and receiving and giving love is what feeds our energy. People who are in vegetative states, on life support machines with no hope of recovery, find that their energy is stuck. So while we do have the ability to keep people alive when they have suffered catastrophic events, it is only their bodies being kept alive and not their souls. But I have faith in the spirit world, so I know that there is another life after this one and I believe that we should trust in the deep spiritual instinct we have and release people when it is their time to go.

The question of what happens spiritually when science and death meet becomes even more interesting when you consider a widely-held prediction of how humans and machines will evolve in the coming decades. Ray Kurzweil is a renowned computer scientist and 'futurist' – he studies current trends and uses them to predict the future. He also advises Google, so he's someone whose views are taken seriously. He predicted that by the mid-2040s humans will have developed technology so advanced and intelligent that it will allow us to overcome obstacles such as illness and, perhaps, even death itself. Man and machine will integrate in both the physical and virtual worlds at a point in history called the singularity. It is a radical idea that sounds like science fiction but one which received a lot of attention and serious consideration.

But if we no longer die, where would that leave us spiritually? How can our energy ever be released? I believe that although the idea is interesting, while humans certainly have an inbuilt desire to prolong life, technology and science will only ever be allowed to delay the inevitable. Death will still be as inevitable as it always has been.

On a biological level, when a person dies their heart stops, their breathing stops, their blood stops circulating and their brain ceases to function. Their body dies, and when it does, their soul passes over into another realm where they live on. We live in a different way. The difference is the body: the form and matter that we need on Earth and which makes us humans is useless in spirit. Our bodies come from nothing and they go to nothing but the energy within them is eternal.

The act of dying itself is not scary at all. At the point in our lives where we stop breathing and our body shuts down, we reach a peaceful place, even if the circumstances are not. Even if someone is murdered, as they die they find peace no matter what the external conditions are. And even though many who pass are aware they are dying and are fearful, they have lucid moments near death when their loved ones come to reassure them. No one dies alone. Even if the person who dies does not know anyone directly in spirit – even if they have no known dead relatives or friends – he or she will still be linked to the afterlife through ancestors who have passed, and that link will enable them to be guided into the spirit world. It is like a chain that stretches back through time. Spirits linked to us come at the point of death because they are familiar to us and they come to reassure us. They have walked the path before, so they come to guide us. They are drawn to us, we don't call them.

The fact that there is always someone waiting for us in spirit was brought vividly to life for me at one of the shows I performed, where two male spirits came through and I knew instinctively that they shared a family connection. They showed me a scene. One of them was lying in a hospital bed surrounded by machines that were keeping him alive. The other man, who was older, was standing at the foot of the bed and a woman was seated by the side of him, sobbing. Three names popped into my head: Ben, Julie and Colin.

I explained all this to the audience and a lady raised her hand. She explained that her name was Julie and that her husband was in spirit and his name was Ben.

"And who is Colin?" I asked.

"He's my father-in-law," she answered.

"He is in spirit?" I asked. She nodded. I explained the hospital scene I was seeing and I felt a build-up of pressure inside my head. I relayed this to Julie who explained that Ben had died from a brain haemorrhage.

The reading was extremely emotional. Julie didn't have to say anything, she just nodded her head in recognition as I described how she had been there at the bedside while her husband lay dying and how, unbeknownst to her at the time, Ben's father Colin had been there waiting to guide his son into the afterlife.

"They are together," I told her. "He didn't die alone. His dad came to get him."

Some souls, however, choose not to go to that place immediately, even when they have a guide. Instead, they choose to stay here. They are not trapped or kept against their will. I believe the journey to the afterlife is like a staircase. You can choose to go all the way up, you can stop halfway or you can stay at the bottom. Souls who choose to stay, and to show themselves as ghosts, have different reasons for their actions. Lucky, the New England ghost, for example, was from New York, and was a wayward child. I imagine she had a horrific childhood up until the time she was sent to Westport, which in the fifties would have seemed like paradise to a girl like her. Even though she was deeply troubled and she died, I feel she would have wanted to stay there because for a girl from her background, a big house by the sea would have seemed close to heaven.

There's another destination that souls can take in the afterlife, which you might be surprised by. They can come back and inhabit another body. It's a process you'll likely know as reincarnation. It differs from possession, which is when a malevolent spirit purposely takes over the body of a living person. Reincarnation is the idea that a soul is reborn in a fresh body to live another life. The soul doesn't remember its former life, although at points it might have glimpses of recognition, which is how we explain déjà vu.

The word reincarnation literally means 'to take flesh again' and is a commonly held belief in many eastern religions such as Hinduism, Jainism and Buddhism. It's been debated around the world from India to Greece, and there are references to it in ancient texts dating back to the sixth century BC. Some religions believe that souls are required to take a progressive journey through multiple lives and are reborn into new bodies after death depending on what they did in their previous incarnations. So, if you were a good horse, you might come back as a human, or if you were a bad human, you might come back as a dog (although I'd happily come back as my dogs, which are spoilt rotten).

In some versions of reincarnation, a soul can come back as a plant. The whole 'birth rebirth repeat' cycle can get incredibly complicated when the idea of reincarnation is viewed through a religious prism. Take Hinduism, for example. There, it is believed a soul or spirit, after biological death, resides in a counterpart of the physical body called the astral body which is made of astral matter and resides in a parallel world. At the right time it begins a new life in a new body that may be human or animal depending on the moral quality of the previous life's actions. This is all governed by karma and in order to escape the cycle of birth and death a soul must seek higher forms of happiness through spiritual experience. When, after a lot of spiritual meditation and training, a person realizes that the true 'self' is the immortal soul rather than the body or the ego, all desires for the pleasures of the world vanish and the person will not be born again and will instead spend eternity in a place of peace and happiness, or heaven, known as Loka. There they join in the company of the Supreme Being.

Every religion that believes in reincarnation has their own version. Sikhism has similar beliefs to Hinduism in that a soul is passed from life to life and the actions of the previous life determine the type of body the soul is born into.

Buddhist belief differs. Followers believe everything is one constant flow of consciousness that links one life to the next and that death starts a new life, like the flame of a dying candle being used to light a new one. The consciousness in the new person is different from that in the deceased but the two form a continual stream.

I'm not sure that we do travel through body after body in an attempt to reach spiritual enlightenment. I think our journeys in the afterlife are sometimes guided by a higher power and are preordained, but I think we can choose where we go to a degree and ultimately end up where we should be. Think of it like a journey being guided by sat nav. Your destination is established before you set off but you are free to divert if you fancy a change of scenery, or if a road is closed ahead. Ultimately, you still get to the end point, you just take a different route. This applies in life and death. Everyone goes when it is their time, but they get to choose how they reach that final destination and they choose their journey in the next life.

I also think what happens in life is mapped out for us. Life is full of coincidences which suggest there is a plan and that we are following a blueprint that has been designed for us. Take identical twins for example. There are many stories of identical twins being separated at birth and going off to live with different families without contact. But when they are reunited in later life it transpires that their lives have followed very similar paths. They've married people with the same name, done similar jobs, they have the same taste in music and clothes and have had similar life experiences. It is almost as if they have been following a predetermined path. As if their lives were mapped out for them before they were born. Maybe something is written into our energy, like a plan but on a deeper level than DNA, something that doesn't just determine physical characteristics but predetermines behaviour and situations and the choices we make.

Reincarnation presents itself in some very weird ways. Some people will have past life regression, in which they are hypnotised to recover memories of past lives. I'm not so sure about this. Not all souls are reincarnated and when it does happen, when a soul settles in a new body, memories get wiped clean, like when you reformat a memory stick, otherwise you wouldn't know what life you were living. Starting afresh in a new body without being encumbered by the memories of your former self is good metaphysical housekeeping. But there are some cases where those memories aren't entirely deleted, which is where déjà vu comes in.

That said, you can tell when a person – especially a young person – is a reincarnated soul. Some people are older than their years. It's not that they know more or can speak and walk earlier and remember things that happened before they were born, they just have a way about them. They seem that little bit more worldly wise. We call them 'old souls'. I've got three daughters and there's no doubt that my youngest is an old soul. She's old beyond her years, not in a physical way but in some indistinct way that's difficult to put a finger on.

I know I've been here before, and there's a reason why I know, which sounds strange but which to me is total validation. It's to do with John's back. Allow me to explain. John is four years older than I am. When we first started our relationship, we were in bed one evening chatting idly and John was lying on his stomach. I remember looking down at him and suddenly thinking very clearly, "I know that back." It was the strangest thing. His back was so familiar, the shape, the muscle tone, the pattern of moles, but I couldn't place where I'd seen it before. I was fascinated by it and ever since, I've had a feeling that I've known his back in another life. That is weird, but it gets stranger.

Many years later I gave birth to my daughter, Fern. I was in the delivery ward immediately after she came out and the doctor showed her to me and then gave her a quick inspection to make sure everything was okay. He turned her over in his hands and I saw her back for the first time. My first thought? "Oh my God, that's John's back." It was the same instinctive feeling that I'd had many years before.

Now, obviously, Fern is John's daughter, so they are likely to share similarities, but I was convinced that I knew that back and in an instant, I felt that in some previous incarnation, I had seen the same back on another child of mine. It was like an incredibly vivid sense of recognition, but I was in another body, looking at this back on a child that I realised was my son. It was just a snatch of memory that lasted a fraction of a second but was so clear it made my head spin.

The upshot of this realisation is that I've married my son, who has come back into my life when we have both inhabited new bodies. I told you it was strange!

Why do some of us come back and some don't? I think we come back here to Earth to learn lessons or to make amends and cleanse our energy until it is pure enough to pass into the afterlife. In rare cases, I believe people who have committed dreadful atrocities like genocide and mass murder in former lives are sent back, but not as another bad soul. I think there's more to the grand plan than a sort of endless cycle of punishment. I suppose what I hope is that these bad souls are somehow 'washed' along the way; that they are purged of their evil. But not everyone sent back has been naughty in another life or done something horrendous. Perhaps when someone died, their energy was not balanced between good and bad, their moral equilibrium was perhaps tipped over into the red because in life they had done slightly more naughty things than good deeds. Maybe in these circumstances a soul gets reincarnated to rebalance the ledger. They can be sent back to learn lessons and to have another crack at living a spiritual life.

Chapter 4

The search for meaning

As anyone who has had a child knows, childbirth is one of the most terrifying, wonderful, life-changing experiences a human body goes through. I'm sure it's just as wonderful and scary for men, but they generally get through it physically unscathed, unless they are the recipient of an emotionally charged well-placed punch or two during the process. The human body is an amazing thing, both spiritually and physically. It can endure more than we give it credit for and has a remarkable ability to heal from trauma of the body and soul. Childbirth is one of the most traumatic events most of us will put our minds and bodies through.

This is probably why, when you get pregnant for the first time, no one really explains the full extent of what will happen to you. They tend to focus on the good bits and don't explain just how painful and traumatic child-birth can be. It's like every mum who had a dramatic first birth (and most do) decides afterwards "I think I'll keep that quiet" whenever they meet a new mum-to-be: a global conspiracy of silence to ensure the future of the human race, because let's face it, if you knew the full facts, you might never have children, and gradually humanity would die out.

Thankfully, in the safe and secure modern Western world in which we live, there are very few times before we reach old age when we are reminded of our own frailties and shortcomings. Generally, we are always in control. We decide what we do and when we do it. Childbirth is one of the rare times when we are no longer in control, no matter how much we like to think we are. No matter how much we plan. I mean, how many carefully plotted and scheduled birth plans have been ripped up and thrown away after the first early contractions. When you are begging for pain relief bent over a yoga ball on the floor of the maternity ward, you stop caring what scent the aromatherapy candles are, or whether there is whale song playing on the Sonos speaker! You just want to get through the process and get the baby out, and when you do get to the other side, you are a changed person. Not only are you a mum, you've also experienced one of the most primal physical processes a body can go through and it changes you on a deep spiritual level.

This is an interesting fact of life because facing trauma and overcoming it can often lead to a form of enlightenment. People have epiphanies in crisis. They come face to face with their mortality, find an inner strength and put faith in a higher power to get them through whatever it is they are facing. Similarly, many people who have had near-death experiences come out the other side with a renewed understanding of their lives and their place in the universe.

I know this to be true because I've spoken to people who have been near death and I've been there myself, during childbirth. And when I did, I felt that higher power. I touched divinity.

I was pregnant with my second child, Rebecca, and went into labour at 32 weeks. This was almost 50 years ago and obstetrics were very different then. Nowadays it wouldn't be unusual at all for a baby to be born several weeks earlier and mums usually get notice when things are not going to plan during the pregnancy. But this was before they had the sophisticated kind of monitoring technology that they do today and so it came as a shock to suddenly go into early labour and be rushed into hospital.

I was trying to stay calm as the staff prodded, poked and scanned.

"There's nothing to be worried about," they told me after what seemed like an eternity of tests, throughout which my contractions were feeling progressively stronger, "but your baby is not quite big enough yet, so we are going to give you something to stop the contractions."

They explained to me that they were going to give me a drug that would affect my heart rate and blood pressure and that it was quite normal in cases of early labour to administer medication to halt things and give the baby's lungs more time to develop in the womb.

What I didn't know at the time was that I was born with what they call a 'normal abnormality' in my heart. I've got what's known as an atrial fibrillation, which basically means my heart beats irregularly every now and then. Sometimes it beats too fast, which is fine normally but does mean I am prone to strokes as I get older and I have a slightly enlarged left chamber.

I know all this now, but back then when I was in my mid-twenties they hadn't found that out. I'd had no major health problems up until then and assumed I was a normal healthy young woman, which I was, apart from the iffy ticker.

I was lying on the hospital bed, panicking that something was wrong with my baby, despite the medic's assurances that all would be fine. There were two doctors standing by the side of the bed. I had an IV line in the back of my hand and they connected a syringe to it. One doctor explained that the drug would not knock me out and I'd probably not even notice anything different while the other slowly depressed the plunger to administer the medication. As he did, I remember looking at one of the men and having a sudden, very strong realisation that my life was about to end.

"I'm going to die," I said to him.

He was quite surprised. "No, you're not," he replied with a frown.

The other doctor, who had been administering the drug looked up and said to me, "What did you say?"

But I couldn't answer. I could feel my heart starting to race. I felt warm at first and then felt myself starting to slip away.

I heard one of the men, but it sounded as if he was far away. His voice sounded panicky.

"Her heart rate is climbing too fast," he said.

But I didn't care. I was somewhere else, having an out-of-body experience, and although I knew I was dying, I loved what I was feeling. I felt totally comfortable and at peace, rising out of my body and looking at the scene as if someone else was on the bed. I was drifting away from myself and even though I had two young daughters (and a third on the way) and a husband, I didn't feel an urge to fight what I was feeling. I just accepted it was happening and I gave myself to it. I felt love and comfort. I was warm, like someone had poured warm water over me. I was totally unaware of the mayhem that was taking place around me as the medics fought to reverse the effects of the drug and bring me back to the land of the living. I could feel another presence waiting somewhere just out of view.

My last thought as I drifted away was, "I'm going to live here, it's beautiful." And then bang! I was back in hospital. They'd given me an antidote to counteract the effects of the drug that was causing my heart to go haywire.

I felt groggy and unsure of where I was for several minutes. I couldn't remember how I got there. And then the details started to come back to me.

"You gave us quite a scare," said one of the doctors.

"I was dying," I whispered.

The drugs they gave me obviously had an effect, but they were not drugs designed to have an effect on my mental state, so I can only surmise that the blissful feeling

I had in my near-death experience was how death feels. Some religious people experiencing the same would no doubt say they were in the presence of God. I know I felt spirit in its purest form. I was nearer to divinity than I had ever been, and it felt wonderful.

It was very different to the feeling I have when I connect to spirit to give people readings. In those instances, I know there's someone connected with me from the spirit world, and I can feel their energy. Sometimes I can get spooked by what I'm shown or what I feel. Sometimes it can be unpleasant (although spirit means me no harm). In those situations, I also always have control. This was very different. It was all-encompassing and I didn't feel alone or scared. I was dying and I fully accepted it.

That experience has stuck with me all these years and whenever I recall it, I get an enormous sense of peace because I'm not scared of death. I know what happens, I know how it feels.

Many people who have been through something similar will say the same, that there is nothing to be scared about. I count myself lucky to have had a near-death experience because it has allowed me to draw back the curtains and have a sneaky preview of a process that we all fear. And we do, because no matter how much I could tell you that there is nothing to be frightened of, and that even if you experience a painful death, it is only fleeting and what comes afterwards is beautiful, it is still human nature to be terrified of dying. All animals have an innate survival instinct that ensures we'll do almost anything to stay alive. Perhaps there is a reason for this. Maybe, if the truth were known, that we live on and that death is a lovely experience, we'd all pack up and do ourselves in at the first sign of hardship.

So why are we so scared of death?

The main reason is because as far as many believe, it is final. You die and are no longer here in your physical form; there's no coming back, which is weird for me to say because I know there is life after death and that some of us even come back here, to the Earth plane, to live other lives. But I've spent my lifetime explaining this to people and shown thousands of people the possibility of spirit and there is still a long way to go before everyone believes.

For those who hope there's something else, but are not sure, there is fear of the unknown. Others assume death always means pain and suffering.

Some, who may have done bad things in life, fear death because they worry it leads to some form of judgement and punishment. When people ask me about hell in the afterlife, I tell them not to worry, because there is plenty of hell here on Earth. Not the great lakes of fire and eternal damnation version of hell. It is a hell compared to what follows.

Another big reason why most people fear death is because they assume they will no longer see or be with their loved ones. That's a terrifying thought for anyone. I know that if I could never see my kids or my grand-children again, I would not be able to survive. There are other reasons, too. Some people fear death because they want to achieve more in life. Some people want to leave a mark or a legacy and fear dying before they can achieve that goal. Others fear leaving unfinished business.

For these reasons I understand why people fear death. But I know that when I die, the actual process whereby my heart stops and I take my final breath is going to be completely pain free, even if it happens when I'm under-neath a bus. I know I'm going to be on another journey by that point and if it's anything like the experience I had in the hospital when I was giving birth, it will be wondrous.

* * *

This certainty is what faith is all about and faith is an important element of your spirit energy. It's one of the keys to unlock your spiritualism. Knowing that there is a certainty in life after death is just one way that faith helps us navigate through life and boosts our energy.

But it's not just faith in an afterlife that enriches spirituality. Faith can be a superpower against negativity in all walks of life. It doesn't solve every problem and it would be foolish and naive to expect that you can get through life and achieve success and happiness with faith alone, but faith certainly allows you to focus on the positives and helps you make decisions based on positive instincts.

Faith sometimes gives you the extra shove you need to take that step into the unknown and be brave. You'll find that, usually, if you put your faith in instinct and take the plunge, things work out in your favour. I've made some of the most important decisions of my life based on faith, even when, at the time, they seemed rash. My decision to become a professional medium was, on the face of it, impulsive and random, but I put my faith in the decision and knew at the time that I was being guided by spirit.

It happened back in the early eighties when I was a young mother working as a dental nurse. I loved my job and would have happily carried on were it not for a disagreement with the wife of the head dentist at the practice, who also happened to be the practice manager. We didn't get on, maybe she took an exception to me because I was always happy, friendly and often had a laugh with her husband. I think that maybe she suspected he liked me in more than a professional capacity and maybe he did. I don't know. I was young and naive and perfectly happy with John. But one day she called me about some admin and we ended up having terse words because I was accused of something or other that I hadn't done. The row escalated and I probably said some things I shouldn't have.

In hindsight, I could have been slightly more diplomatic and, rather than diffuse the situation, my boldness just enflamed it. She went bonkers again and started calling me all kinds of names. And that's when my faith whispered in my ear and told me to get the hell out of there.

"You know what," I thought to myself, "stuff your job!" But before I had a chance to say it, I was sacked and told to leave.

I turned and walked out and never looked back. I got in my car but, once the adrenaline rush had subsided, I thought to myself, "What am I going to do now?"

I had a young family and we needed two incomes. John was a greengrocer at the time and money was tight. We needed every penny that came our way.

It was mid-afternoon and I'd only been gone for a few hours when I got home. John had done the early shift at the shop, having done the market run in the early hours, so he'd finished for the day and was in the kitchen reading the paper when I walked in.

"What are you doing back so early?" he asked.

"I've left my job."

"What?" he frowned.

I explained what had happened. He laughed at the image of me standing up for myself and giving as good as I got.

"Love, we need the money. You'll have to go back and apologise. I'm sure he'll take you back. Just flutter your eyelashes at him," he joked.

"No way." I was resolute.

"But we can't get by on my wages alone," he said. "What are we supposed to do?"

My faith intervened again.

"I'm going to be a medium," I stated.

Up until then, I had been doing readings for friends and a few friends of friends at the weekends and on occasional evenings, but it was only ever for pin money or in exchange for favours.

"Full time," I finished.

John was doubtful. "What? You reckon you can get enough clients to earn a full-time wage?" he quizzed.

But I was adamant. I had complete faith that I could make a go of my new, hastily hit-upon working life. And then something really weird happened. The phone rang. And this is the honest truth. I answered it and there was a woman on the other end of the line.

"Is that Sally Morgan?" she asked.

"Yes," I said, not recognising the voice.

She explained that I had been recommended to her by a friend who I had done a couple of readings for.

"I'm in the area for the next few days for the tennis at Wimbledon," she explained. "I was wondering if you'd have time to see me for a reading?"

You could have knocked me down with a feather.

"Yes of course," I blurted. While this was going on, John was looking at me puzzled.

"How much do you charge?" the lady asked.

My previous rate had been a few quid here and there, or a bunch of flowers.

"It's £25 for an hour," I said, plucking a figure out of the air.

"That would be great," she said, so becoming my first client as a professional. By the end of the week, I had others booked in too. Word soon spread. I never even had to advertise, I just paid for a listing in the Yellow Pages under Mediums and Clairvoyants. I've never looked back.

Faith may not have led her to me, but it undoubtedly

gave me the courage I needed to take the leap and make the right decision – I guess that's why it's called a leap of faith.

Faith can make the scary seem less frightening. It can give us that extra nudge we need or boost our confidence enough to get us through a tough patch.

We all needed faith during the pandemic. Faith in the vaccine has got us through and while faith is not a cure, having faith in the ability of the scientists who developed the vaccines means that millions of us have been jabbed, which has enabled life to get back to some sort of normality.

I needed to call on my faith again at the start of the pandemic, much as millions of others did. At the start of 2020 I was looking forward to another year on the road, with over 90 dates booked on my tour. It was March and I'd finished a show somewhere in the South West. It had been a brilliant night. I was with a couple of members of the crew and we were driving back home to Surrey. All the talk was about this strange flu-like illness that people were catching. I'd been following the news and although I was concerned, I assumed that it would be under control soon. That night, just before midnight, one of the crew got a message from the theatre we were due to perform in the following night.

"They've cancelled," he said. And my initial thought

was, "That's handy, I've got a night off." But as the week went on, more and more venues cancelled. And then lockdown happened. First, we assumed theatres would go dark for a few weeks, then a month. Then six weeks. Slowly, every one of the thousands of people who work in the theatre industry realised that life was going to get very tough and that the curtains were staying down for the foreseeable future.

I could have gone into meltdown. My income ended overnight. I was unable to pay my crew. But I maintained faith. I trusted that everything would be okay and I had faith in my ability to work through the problem.

At this point, there is a very important distinction to make between faith and blind faith. For the past decade or so there has been a trendy self-help movement which subscribes to the idea that if you imagine something hard enough it will happen: because you've imagined it so much, you've attracted it to you. This theory circumvents the idea that if you want something in life, you have to work hard for it.

Blind faith has no vision and fate intervenes in every life. Faith has limits. You can't change destiny or external events unrelated to you with faith alone. You can't sit back in life and expect everything you wish for to happen to you just because you wish it so. You need to get your hands dirty sometimes. What faith does allow you is the space and psychological strength to act in a rational way, or find solutions when problems arise. It puts fear in check and while fear can be a very useful human emotion, it can often cloud judgement and stop us seeing a way forward. Developing faith in a positive outcome, be that metaphysical faith in an afterlife or faith in your own earthly abilities, is a powerful spiritual ability. It's part of the spirit energy toolkit. And sometimes, just sometimes, you may find that fate does intervene, as it did for me.

We had been trying to sell our house for two years and within a month of the first lockdown happening, a family that had looked at it 18 months previously came back and bought it, which gave us enough financial breathing space to survive while I established my online service.

* * *

Faith attracts spiritual energy. Every person of faith I've met has a certain aura of peace and positivity that I believe spirits are drawn to. As an example, several years ago I was visited on numerous occasions by a young man who was in training to be an imam. I had no idea that was his profession when he booked, and only realised when he arrived dressed in a white shalwar kameez.

To be honest, I was surprised at first that a Muslim

would be interested in my work, but he explained that he was there out of curiosity and that while Islam does not believe in ghosts, it does believe that people have souls and spirits and the Qur'an also mentions jinns, which are invisible beings of great physical strength. He wanted to investigate what mediums did, which I took as a compliment.

He came for about six readings and was a fascinating character, a lovely, warm, gentle man. At each reading I could feel his energy radiating out like a warm glow. I think it was something to do with his natural curiosity and openness. It attracted spirit to him and so, naturally, the readings I gave him were accurate, which gave him much cause for thought. We became friends and on one occasion he bought me a gift, which was a gold desk plaque engraved with what I assumed was Arabic writing. He explained that it was a traditional blessing and would protect me from any evil.

The last time I saw him he arrived with a much older man, who was dressed in a white robe and appeared much more serious and stern. My friend explained that this was a senior member of his local mosque and that he had brought him along to witness my abilities. The older man barely looked me in the eye and would not speak to me directly. It made for an awkward reading and when they left I never saw or heard from my friend again. I suspect the senior imam did not approve of his psychic research project.

But every religion seeks answers to what happens in the afterlife and every single religion believes in an afterlife. Every mainstream religion (except Buddhism) believes in a god of some sort or a higher power. Even Pagans believe in a higher power. Spirituality often gets confused with Paganism, but they are different. Many Wiccans and other Pagans are polytheistic, meaning they honour more than one divine being. Some see all deities as one, and may refer to one god or goddess, while others worship specific gods or goddesses. Some mix and match religious practice. Some Pagans for example will do a bit of witchcraft and then pray to Jesus. Generally, most see the role of god as a job title, rather than an individual.

Spiritualism is another religious movement that gets confused with spirituality. It is a common misunderstanding that spirituality and Spiritualism are the same things, but in reality they are not. Confusingly Spiritualism can often be taken to mean both the belief that there is a reality that cannot be perceived by the senses and the name of the religious movement.

Spiritualism as a religion believes much the same as I do, but practises it in a controlled hierarchy. It believes in spirit entities and that mediums can channel those spirits from the spirit world into the world of the living. Spirituality on the other hand, which we are mainly concerned about in this book, is much more of a personal experience, but which is guided by the energy and hidden powers that we can draw from spirit.

The modern Spiritualism religion traces its beginnings to a series of apparently supernatural events at a farmhouse in Hydesville, New York, in 1848. The owner and his family, as well as the previous occupants of the house, had been disturbed by unexplained knocking noises at night. After a severe disturbance, the owner's youngest daughter, Kate Fox, communicated with the spirit by asking it to rap in relation to the number of fingers she held up, which it did. Kate and the spirit established a 'rapport' (excuse the pun) and together they developed a code which was used to give answers, probably in the form of one knock for yes, two knocks for no. By this process the spirit was said to have identified himself as a man who had been murdered in the house.

Modern Spiritualism is full of colourful characters and stories. Helena Petrovna Blavatsky, for example was the late 19th century's most infamous mystic and medium. Known as Madame Blavatsky, she co-founded the Theosophical Society in 1875, which still exists today. Its aim was to investigate the area where science, religion, and philosophy merges. While living in West Philadelphia, USA, Madame Blavatsky became ill with a seriously infected leg and during a period of delirium underwent a spiritual transformation, which led her to establish the society.

Photographs of her show a wild-haired eccentric Russian woman who was said to enjoy a diverse career as a circus horse rider, a professional pianist, a business-woman and a spiritualist. Legend has it that she trekked through the mountains of Tibet on a spiritual quest for seven years, although no one recorded seeing her there. She is also rumoured to have survived shipwrecks, gunshot wounds and sword fights. She claimed to have discovered a mythical kingdom in the Gobi Desert where eternal beings who ruled the cosmos lived. Clearly, she was a good storyteller.

All religions have different practices and protocols that are supposed to help followers engage with the key elements of the religion and bring them closer to the divine head of the creed being worshipped.

Meditation is a popular way of connection to the higher energy around us and I do agree that regular periods of quiet contemplation can be spiritually enriching. You can go overboard, however. I heard a story a while ago about a monk from somewhere in Asia who sat down outside a special temple he'd gone on a pilgrimage to and started to meditate. He went into a trance and stayed there for weeks with a faint, ecstatic smile on his face. He looked so peaceful people left him alone. It was only when flies were buzzing around him that people realised he'd died. But he looked so happy they just left him there and over time his body mummified. I'm not sure if it's true or not but the message is clear. Meditation can be good but set yourself time limits.

Meditation, religious contemplation and prayer all represent a human desire to search for deeper meaning. Some people try to achieve deeper meaning, or a kind of spirituality, through mind-altering drugs, almost as a way of shortcutting the hard work. Some Native American tribes, for example, use a psychoactive cactus called peyote in their ceremonies. Likewise, marijuana is regarded as a herb of religious significance and used in Rastafari reasoning sessions, which are communal meetings involving meditation. Marijuana is used by Rastafarians to heighten feelings of community and to produce visions.. I'm not sure drugs are the quick answer, though. Maybe they do allow the brain to relax a little bit and the spirit valve to open but it's not something I'd recommend. Besides, if you take LSD and suddenly see your gran who's been dead for 10 years, how would you know it's her spirit, and not a drug-induced hallucination?

Another way spirituality is invoked is through ceremony and language. My profession is guilty of this and it is a constant bugbear of mine. Some mediums will dress their practice up in phrases like "take it with you" after every sentence and "God bless you". I avoid all this nonsense. I believe the work of a psychic should be accessible, natural, ordinary and regular, if only to make it more acceptable. If you start dressing things up with mumbo-jumbo you turn people off and put them on edge. Those fake spiritual people I mentioned before can be guilty of this. You don't have to take your shoes off and sit cross-legged to connect to your hidden spirit energy.

During the pandemic, when times were confused and uncertain, this desire for discovery and answers increased. It's in our nature to look for meaning, particularly when we are fearful. Having faith helps. The drift away from organised religion which has been taking place through-out the last 50 years, however, has sent people looking for answers in all kinds of places. Social media fuelled fertile imaginations with conspiracy, for instance.

Undoubtedly there are big answers out there and things we don't know and will not discover for decades. I sometimes entertain the thought that maybe aliens have visited Earth at some stage, for example, which a lot of people will think is mad. But it would be incredibly arrogant and ignorant of us to think that we're the only beings in the entire universe. And I think that there are government secrets that are kept from us by America, Russia and China. But turning to the kind of conspiracy that you find online about vaccines and global plots to control the human race is crazy. Sometimes you have to be rational (which I know sounds strange coming from a psychic).

The gap between our need for certainty and answers and our drift away from religion should be filled with spirituality. Call it an evolution of faith.

The crisis we have all gone through, both as a species and personally, has exposed our need for something more. On a global scale we are confronted by existential threats: climate change, plastics in the seas, political unrest. It all exposes our vulnerability. We need a renewed sense of hope and we only get that sense of hope from inside by having faith, by being positive and by persevering and working to solve our problems.

During the pandemic everyone wanted to feel connected to each other and in a way we all were, because for the first time in modern history we were all in the same boat and facing a common threat. The common thread that we can all pull upon to build and maintain that connection between us all is our spirit energy.

Chapter 5

Spiritual capital

Joanne came to me because the rest of her family made her. She won't mind me saying that she hated the world and that she was a fairly unpleasant person with a huge chip on her shoulder. She couldn't care less about anyone else or about herself. She was in a deep pit of despair, and she had every reason to be.

Two years before, she had hit rock bottom and was sent to see me because she had lost her only son, Jake. He had been training as a solicitor and, after several years learning and getting experience at a provincial law firm, he had recently landed a job at a big city firm. He was finally going places and Joanne and her husband Robin couldn't have been more pleased. Then, two weeks before his 23rd birthday, Jake was killed in a hit-and-run accident while walking home one night after a meal out with friends. Initially he was in a coma, but when, after a week in intensive care, the neurologists told Joanne and Robin that their son was brain dead, they made the agonising decision to turn off his life support.

Jake had been a mummy's boy. Every birthday Joanne took him to a West End show. It was his guilty pleasure. On the day Joanne was supposed to be seeing *Tina: The Musical* with her son, she sat at home with a bottle of gin and contemplated suicide. She never recovered from losing him and the grief never subsided. Some days it hurt so much all she could do was lay in bed and wait for it to pass. The driver of the car eventually came forward and admitted what he'd done. His court case and causing death by dangerous driving conviction gave Joanne no closure. Instead, the negativity and pain started to fester. It was like an infected wound that could never heal. She started to drink.

Robin tried to help but he too was fighting his own battle. As often happens in tragedy, the couple pulled apart, rather than pulling together. No one could say or do anything that would make it better, because Jake was never coming back.

To start with, Joanne assumed the shakes she was experiencing were down to the booze. She told me that when, 18 months after Jake's death, she was diagnosed with Parkinson's, she was relieved.

"I hope it's quick," she thought to herself.

Fate works in mysterious ways, and it did for Joanne. Her sister had been to see a couple of my shows and was impressed by what I did. When the pandemic hit and the shows stopped, I started to do online readings. Joanne's sister followed me on social media, saw I was doing one-on-one readings and told Joanne.

I'm not sure how she persuaded her to get in touch with me but she did, and when we first met, via Zoom, it's fair to say Joanne was in a very dark place. She didn't care about herself or anyone else for that matter. You didn't need to be psychic to see that she was in pain, but I could feel it in her energy. Grief infects people.

"Oh darling," I said when I saw her on the screen, "it's been awful, hasn't it?"

To start with she had looked quite defiant, as if she didn't want to engage, but when I said this I could see the corners of her eyes soften.

"Yes," she said.

I was feeling a strong pull of energy from spirit, and I knew there was a young man who was trying to connect with her. In my mind I heard a phrase.

"This is coming through to me, it's quite random," I admitted, "but do the words 'he is young, let him rest' mean anything to you?"

Her eyes immediately welled up and her composure cracked.

I heard more words in my mind, and distant music.

"Bring him home," I frowned.

She was nodding and crying. She could barely get the words out.

"*Les Mis*," she said.

I was confused.

"The musical?" I asked.

She nodded.

Then, I sensed a theatre and laughter. I saw the lady and a young man together in a city at night. And I heard a name.

"Who is Jack, or Jake?" I asked.

"My son," she sobbed.

As the reading went on it was like she was thawing. Her defences came down and she allowed herself to have faith in what was happening. In doing so the connection between her and her son became stronger and the messages I was receiving became clearer. It created a feedback loop and by the end of the hour she was a very different woman. I could feel the relief in her.

"I just needed to know he is okay," she said.

"He is at peace," I told her truthfully. "He is surrounded by love and he is always close to you and in your heart.

He never suffered and he doesn't want you to suffer either."

Joanne saw me on two other occasions and by the time we said our final goodbye we had built up a bond.

"I need to get on with my life, don't I Sally?" she said the last time we spoke.

"You need to live for yourself and to create a new future for yourself," I said. "It will never stop hurting but the pain changes and you will learn to cope. Of course, you'll miss him every day, but say his name, remember him and he'll send you signs so you know he is always there."

The last I heard, Joanne had started to work as a volunteer for a young person's charity and had found renewed purpose in her life. Her son had saved her from herself.

Why am I telling you this?

Joanne's story is a perfect example of something I call 'spiritual capital' in action. Spiritual capital is the currency we need to live spiritually meaningful lives. We gain this capital by living a certain way and adopting certain behaviours. Spiritual capital accumulates within us, strengthening our spirit energy. Think of it like paying money into a bank account or collecting Clubcard points. The more spiritual capital you accumulate, the wealthier you become – not in a financial sense, but in a psychological and spiritual sense.

Spiritual capital

Two of the key elements of spiritual energy are positivity and faith (which we discussed in the previous chapter). These help you see life in a certain way. They allow you to focus on the good.

To put it another way, if you are permanently angry, depressed, hateful and cynical, your attention will always be focused on the negative and it won't matter whether good things happen or not, because you will not be able to see them. Life, as I've mentioned, is always a balance between good and bad. There will always be bad things, but we can choose how we let them affect us, up to a point. Joanne was so focused on the bad things that had happened to her, she was blinkered to anything good. In this mindset, no matter what good things happened, she was unable to see them.

When she changed perspective and started paying spiritual capital into her account, she was able to build up her spirit energy reserves, look after her well-being and start living a meaningful life again.

* * *

Joanne's story is a metaphor for the world. In the past few years we've gone through a series of shocks and upheavals that threaten to impoverish us all spiritually. From the divisiveness of Brexit to the fear of climate change and the Covid pandemic. Negativity appears to be in the ascendancy.

It would be easy and understandable to focus on these things and retreat from life in fear. The world can increasingly seem like quite an unkind place full of extremes. But extremes exist on a spectrum and, in general, things eventually pull back to the centre because usually, in times of crisis and hardship, that's when we see the best in people. Heroes are born out of disaster. When we have something as extreme as a global pandemic, we see millions of people helping those that are really suffering because of it. The worst often brings out the best in people. So, while it can be understandable to look at the pandemic and lament that life will be worse because of it, we can also change perspective and focus on the good that has come out of it in abundance.

History tells us that following a global crisis there is often a golden period. After the Black Death there was the Renaissance, after the First World War and the Spanish flu epidemic we had the roaring twenties and after the Second World War the West experienced the longest period of peace in history.

We are already experiencing positive changes now. Work patterns are changing, work/life balances are being prioritised and the realisation of the links between

Spiritual capital

environmental damage, disease and economic activity will no doubt better inform future development. But beyond these, we can also expand our spiritual horizons and welcome in a golden age of spirituality.

One of the best ways of doing this is by rebuilding positive connections to other people. We've spent a long time locked away, fearful of contact with others, and it is still very prudent to be careful and social distance where necessary, but as we start to reconnect, it is very important to be mindful of the love we feel and to cherish and acknowledge the simple pleasure of just being able to visit friends, family and neighbours.

Starting to appreciate others again will build a strength of connection that is born of spirit energy. When people connect, their energy connects too. I feel it all the time when I am touring and there are families and groups of friends in the audience. I can feel the energy between them, like a magnetic force. It's why humans are social animals. We are hardwired to be together. And when you have big groups of people, enjoying themselves together in the same place over time, those places absorb some of that energy. It's why when you walk into theatres and some places of worship you feel a positive atmosphere.

You don't have to be a medium to feel it. It has happened to us all. Even the biggest cynic or sceptical non-believer has gone into a room and thought, "I don't like the atmosphere in here." Likewise, we've all been in situations surrounded by people and thought, "This is bloody amazing." In these situations, we are harnessing each other's energy or the energy of the people who have been there before and have laughed together, or cried together or loved together. They've left some of their spiritual capital behind, like coins falling down the back of seats.

Not everyone has the luxury of being able to socialise in person. There are still people in high-risk categories and for them social media and video conferencing, which has evolved massively, offers a vital lifeline.

We've all been living in the digital space to some degree or another and, like the physical world, there is good and bad. While the anti-vaxxers and the trolls will always be there, social media does bring out the goodness in others and gives people a chance to connect. The great thing about social media is that you can block people or just choose not to look at their messages or engage with them. The voice of good is far stronger than the voice of hate.

Even though we are dealing with a digital realm, you can still behave in a spiritual way online and build your spiritual currency.

Rule number one is to be kind. Don't judge, and don't feed the trolls – by that, I mean do not get drawn into the cycle of negativity that often exists when people are discussing controversial or divisive issues. And if you give oxygen to trolls and to people that want to comment in a very detrimental, unrealistic way, you encourage them. They can't hurt you if you don't let them. Sometimes the best way to deal with it is to laugh.

For example, I often get sent photographs of specific parts of the male anatomy – I believe the youngsters call them dick pics! They come from the same 'fan' (I can tell it's him by the size, poor bloke) and he often accompanies his pictures with lurid descriptions of what he plans to do to me. He tells me he loves my butt. He's quite obsessed. I could be horrified and offended, but when you are in the public eye it comes with the territory and the best way I feel I can deal with it is to just laugh about it. My daughter takes the mikey and tells me there are men out there who fantasise about old ladies.

It's very different from when I started working as a medium and the worst thing I had to worry about was a heavy breather who used to leave messages on my answerphone. Nowadays everyone is contactable all the time and everything is instant. But the one thing which cannot be instant is our own spirituality. That is a journey that we are all on, even me. It is an ongoing process which takes a bit of effort and a shift in outlook.

*   *   *

What are the benefits of building your spiritual capital? This seems like an obvious question to those who are spiritual but not religious. Spirituality is about exploring the goodness of what it means to be human, it's about attempting to lead a purer life without having to adhere to the doctrines of a religion. Which is a worthy philosophy, but let's be honest, most us want some sort of return on our spiritual investment. So, what do you get when you cash in your loyalty points? Quite simply you become a better version of yourself and build your spiritual energy, which in turn becomes a kind of force field that protects you against negativity.

Becoming more spiritual can help boost your physical and mental health. If you follow the points I set down in the following chapters you can improve your relationships, your confidence and your happiness levels. You will become more positive and more at peace with yourself and the world. If you have a day where you increase your spiritual capital, you go to sleep with a smile on your face.

Developing your spiritual capital is like exercising. It takes some effort to begin with, but eventually it becomes a habit which makes you stronger. It's like the muscle in your arm. The more you use it, the more effective it becomes.

People often come to me and say, "I want to be a medium, but I'll never be like you." And I reply that while we are all unique and no two people are truly alike, we've still all got the same muscles and so if we use the same weights every day in the same way we'd be able to lift the same things. What I'm trying to say in a roundabout way is that we all have the ability, we just need the know-how.

The secret of unlocking our secret spirit power and building up our spiritual capital is through developing elements of our own personality. Faith is one, and another is honesty. This does not just apply to honesty with other people, by being honest when we admit how many biscuits we've had, or how many glasses of Prosecco, or whether we really do want to go to the work Chrimbo do. It relates to being honest with ourselves. And this is particularly important and poignant in the digital age, because social media makes it easier than ever to be false. Like it or not, we live in a world of instant gratification and manipulation where we can present to the world versions of ourselves that our nearest and dearest wouldn't recognise.

The key here is to be genuine and authentic. Don't spend your time and energy trying to be someone you are not, or comparing yourself to others who you are envious of. You'll end up losing sight of the positives you have in your own life. And I can guarantee that every influencer you long to be like, because they are living their best life on Insta, has exactly the same sort of problems and insecurities as you – probably more.

Over the decades, I've been lucky enough to read for celebrities and royalty. I've heard the secrets of some of the world's biggest stars. And while I would never divulge the confidences I have been privy to, I can categorically say that even those who live public lives beyond the dreams of avarice have the same hang-ups as you and I. As someone wise once said, money doesn't buy happiness, it just buys you a better class of unhappiness.

You shouldn't spend your life trying to be like someone else, but learn to love who you are and what you look like. It is so easy today to put a filter on a photo so people don't know what you really look like, and this is all fine when it's a bit of fun, but some people become consumed by presenting the perfect public face and lose sight of who they really are. Showbusiness was always a world of pretend and make believe and everyone knew that, but now that world seems to be leaching into the real world through social media, creating another pandemic – this time one of insecurity, anxiety, depression and mental health problems.

If you live in a make-believe world long enough, you believe it and it becomes unhealthy for the mind and for the spirit.

Think about some of the most spiritual people you know. My spiritual heroes are Ghandi, Desmond Tutu and Deepak Chopra. I can't ever imagine them using Instagram photo filters to enhance their appearances.

You may start to show the world a different representation of yourself, because that's what everyone else is doing. We all like to think we are individual and independent, but the reality is that we are drawn together by a shared culture. We follow trends and fashion because that's what everyone else in our groups are doing. It goes back to a deep human urge to be part of the pack. We have a need to be accepted and to fit in. That was fine back in cavemen and cavewomen times when the hunters needed to form group bonds so they could work together to hunt prey, and the carers stayed back in the villages and needed to form bonds in order to share tasks effectively. Everyone needed to be accepted because they relied on the group, and if they were cast out, they died.

The human brain developed that need for acceptance, and although we no longer need to hunt woolly mammoths or scavenge for firewood and berries, that part of the human brain is still active. In the social media age, it manifests itself as a desire to get followers, or to get likes, and the way to do this is to project to the world what we think people want to see, even if that isn't who we are. Generally, it's what we assume is a better version of ourselves and our lives. The problems start when we begin to hanker after that version of ourselves, or we believe it. It's not authentic and ultimately it will make you miserable. Yet this is where we are as a society.

As a small example, I was sitting in the sunshine outside a café recently having lunch with a friend, and a mother and daughter sat next to us. The mother looked to be in her fifties, the daughter was in her late teens or early twenties and was a typical young woman with a bronzed tan and a carefully applied full face of contoured make-up. They'd been shopping and the daughter was talking about starting a new job at an estate agent and telling her mother that before she started, she wanted to get hair extensions and a tattoo. Her mother was gently trying to explain to her that perhaps people would make judgements about her if she went into work on her first day looking glammed up, and that the look she should be going for was smart and professional. The daughter argued that the man who interviewed her had a full sleeve of tattoos and that it wasn't unusual at the firm for young staff to have tattoos or hair extensions. That's how young people are, she explained. She was probably right.

And then the food arrived. The daughter had ordered a cod goujon sandwich with a side of chips, the mother had ordered a Greek salad. The daughter picked up her phone, swapped the plates and asked her mother to take a photo of her with the salad that she could then post on social media.

"Can't have people thinking I'm unhealthy," she said.

It struck me as very sad on many levels. Who's judging people for having a posh fish finger sandwich for lunch? Why are people worried about what other people think of their menu choices? What is the girl gaining by posing with a salad, rather than a sandwich?

It seems like such a small thing, but it's a metaphor for how a lot of young people (and increasingly, older people) are living two lives: their real ones and their idealised online ones. The disconnect between the two is growing and the space in between gets filled with misery.

So, is the answer a total withdrawal from social media? Will that make you more spiritual? Stepping away from it occasionally will do no one any harm and getting some perspective on it is always beneficial. But let's face it, deleting our Instagram accounts will not make us holy monks overnight. Most of us will likely never attain that level of spirituality. What we really need to strive for is authenticity. Be who you are, stop chasing idealised versions of yourself and learn to love the person you are. Be realistic about the person you can be. Strive for realistic spirituality.

If we are realistic about our spirituality, we find that when we do actually attain a moment, a split second, where we truly connect with spirit energy and get a glimpse into the spirit world, when we get a sign or connect with a loved one, it is mind blowing.

You know, you don't have to have a near-death experience to feel divinity.

As humans we are unique, so we all have unique spirit energy. And because of this, the way we experience our spirit energy, and the way it expresses itself, will also be unique to the individual. The spirit energy that sits inside each of us waiting to be activated is like a fingerprint or a snowflake. No two are the same.

It is something we are all born with. Children are spiritual in a way that most adults aren't. None are born evil because they are all born with pure energy that life hasn't yet altered or dimmed. They have an innate ability to experience the spirit world that gets knocked out of them as they grow old. How many parents have heard their children talk about something they've seen or heard, usually in their bedroom or when they're on their own? Our first instinct is put it down to their imaginations. That's what we tell them as they grow up.

"Ah, that's sweet, haven't you got an active imagination."

While we shouldn't be scaring them, and telling them, "Yes dear, that's a ghost," neither should we be telling them that what they experience is imagined. By doing that, we are closing that valve that allows them to connect to the spirit energy around them. We are conditioning them to ignore or discount the signs they see and hear.

I was incredibly lucky in my upbringing. We didn't go to church. We didn't follow a religion, but when I saw, sensed and heard things, my mum would never discount them, or tell me I was imagining things and being silly. If we were round someone's house and suddenly I blurted out that I could see an old man standing in the room that no one else saw, she would say, "It's okay, she's just like that."

My mum was very open to possibility and was very much a free spirit. She allowed me to develop my spirit energy.

We should enable children to explore and develop their spirituality, and to be aware of things that might not always be easily explainable without scaring them. So, for example, your child might one day exclaim that they are sure somebody called their name when you didn't hear a thing. Rather than discount it, or tell them they are imagining it, gently explain that there's nothing to be afraid of and that sometimes things like that happen.

The good news is that nowadays, more than ever, society is accepting of what we'd probably class as alternative lifestyles. Those seeking a deeper spiritual life and exploring spirituality are no longer considered to be hippies and mocked. Spirituality is taken seriously. Elements of it – self-improvement, mindfulness, meditation, are widely practised. This is great news for everyone because it gives people the space in which to explore that which was previously seen as a fringe interest.

Attaining fulfilment is a noble pursuit, because increasingly spirituality is quite rightly linked with well-being. It's far more acceptable and becoming even more so. This is another example of the balance in the universe that I talk about. On one end of the spectrum the digital world is drawing some people further from their spirit energy than they've ever been, but at the other end there is genuine openness, acceptance and movement towards spirituality. These changes have happened in my lifetime and continue to happen. The term well-being is now mainstream and widely understood; not so long ago it was seen as a bit weird and only understood by people who lived in communes. The same applies to veganism. What was once seen as niche is now mainstream.

Spiritual capital

Spirituality is a journey that we are all on. Some of us are more aware of it than others. Some of us have a destination in mind and know how to get there; for others, it's more like one of those car rides where, just for the pleasure, you set off with no specific destination in mind.

Chapter 6

The six keys to unlock your spirit power

Beginning

So far, we've learned about spirit energy: what it is, where it comes from, how it benefits us and how it links us to the world beyond our dimension. We've seen that if we can enhance our spirit energy by building spiritual capital, we can become more spiritual.

We've discovered that fate plays a role in our lives and that we are all on a journey with a pre-set destination but where free will allows us to set our own course to reach the end point. We've heard how the hidden mysteries of spirit energy bond our world to the next and can be used to explain some of the amazing, fantastical events documented through history, and through our own lives.

We've discovered that we all possess a well of spirit energy that resides in us and feeds our soul and that we can build and strengthen this energy to help us on our journey through life. While we are all born with our own spirit energy, there are behaviours and life choices we can make that will exercise and grow that energy to make it stronger and more effective. When that happens you become a better, happier, more balanced person, and you become more open to the world of spirit. You become more aware of other people and more attuned to the world, both physically and spiritually. You will find that your relationships with others improve and that your life becomes more positive.

On a metaphysical level I can't promise that you will develop mediumship abilities or attain a transcendent level of inner peace and tranquillity, but I can assure you that you'll be more attuned to the spirit world and will notice the signs and signifiers that indicate the spirit world more.

In this chapter I am going explain about the key qualities, behaviours and elements that you can introduce into your life that will boost your spirit energy and lead to a new, more spiritual version of you. Then, I'll explain how your boosted spirit energy can interact with different areas of your life; finally I'll give you some key exercises you can do which will help you on your quest for enhanced spirit energy.

Although many readers will know me from my theatre tour and my TV shows, you may not know too much about my early life and what led me to become a medium. So, this is my CV, just to let you know you are in expert hands as we delve deeper into the world of spirit energy.

My journey started at a young age when it was quite obvious that I wasn't like the other children. At school I was called "Spooky Sal" because of all the spirits I could talk to.

For the other children and teachers, I was a novelty, but at home, my abilities were just seen as part of who I was. This was probably on account of my grand-mother, Nanny Gladys, who was an amazing woman and could do amazing things. She was a medium, and where we lived (when it was a poor working-class place, not like it is now), she was known as the Witch of Fulham. She ran a newspaper stall outside Putney Bridge Underground station and was one of the lynch-pins of the community. If you wanted to know what Mrs Jones from the laundrette had been up to, Nanny Gladys had the gossip. If you wanted to know who the strange man who visited number 42 was when the man of the house was at work, Nanny Gladys would be able to tell you. She would know things about people that she shouldn't have known. Just by brushing someone's hand when they passed her money for their evening paper, she'd be able to tell deeply personal things about them.

From what my mum told me, Nanny Gladys didn't hide the truths she knew. If someone was up to no good, she'd tell them. If they had a health problem, she'd wish them well. "Hope those piles clear up Norma," she'd say, and then probably put her hand over her mouth in mock shock and try to hide the sparkle in her eye. She was a mischievous one was Gladys and even though she upset plenty of people with her inexplicable knowledge, and scared just as many, she was well thought of in our neighbourhood. Because of her, my early experiences with spirit were seen as nothing unusual and I wasn't discouraged from talking about them or conditioned to believe they were all in my imagination.

When I was 15, I had my first experience of public mediumship when I accompanied my mother to a Spiritualist meeting to test out my 'knowings' (as she called them). There I met some Spiritualists and they encouraged me to give what became the first public demonstration of my gift.

I continued giving private readings to friends and neighbours and built up a reputation for accuracy and for being down-to-earth and approachable. I've never believed in dressing up my abilities, because they are natural. As discussed previously, I eventually had faith in my destiny and made the decision to become a professional medium and started a small practice from home. Word-of-mouth spread and fate intervened again when a member of the royal staff came to see me and was so impressed with what I did, that she told her co-workers, who told their bosses. Eventually someone close to the Princess of Wales came for a reading and recommended me to the Princess herself. Word continued to spread, without me advertising it, and I was soon seeing all manner of famous people, including George Michael and Uma Thurman. I was given my own TV show, *Star Psychic*, which led to a theatre tour and the series *Psychic Sally on the Road*.

A decade of touring the length and breadth of the country followed, with more TV shows and newspaper columns along the way. I started my own psychic school, wrote books and went into the *Celebrity Big Brother* house.

Now, here I am, helping you to realise your potential and see through an incredible window into the wonders of spirit energy. And to do this, you need to incorporate the following key elements into your life.

The six keys to unlock your spirit power

Faith

We have already looked at the role of faith in previous chapters. For the purposes of enhancing spirit energy, the concepts of faith and trust are interchangeable and work on two levels. First you should have faith in spirit. You need to trust that it exists and that there are signs in the world around you that are sent from the spirit world. Without the faith that spirit exists, and that there is a lifeforce of spirit energy that connects everything together, you will never be able to take those glimpses into the world beyond ours and you will never be able to follow the signs that are sent to help guide and support you, or to show you that there is love for you from a world beyond this one. Without faith you would be like an aircraft designer who doesn't believe in the laws of physics trying to invent a plane. It is just not going to work.

Without faith you miss the chance to connect not only to spirit, but to the spirit energy of others. As an example, during my theatre shows I would often get messages from spirit for people in the audience which went unclaimed. On occasion I would be on stage, under the spotlight, explaining to the audience what I was feeling, and I'd know 100 per cent that the message was meant for someone there. I would be able to feel the frustration in the energy I was channelling and sometimes I'd literally be begging for the person the message was meant for to put their hand up and receive it. Eventually, when no connection was made, the energy would fade and the message would go, which always saddened me, because I knew someone, for whatever reason, had missed their chance for a moment of magic.

And then, inevitably, in the line-up to meet the audience and sign books after the show, or in an email a day later, someone would shyly tell me that they believed the unclaimed message was for them, but they were a bit unsure or too embarrassed to take it at the time. In these situations (and there have been hundreds), a little bit of faith would have made a massive amount of difference.

Secondly, faith and trust work on a personal, inward level. It is important to have faith in yourself. Intuition helps you here. It is a powerful tool and is something we are all born with. It's part of our spiritual toolkit. We have thoughts and feelings about people and situations – this is our spirit energy informing us; it is our natural intuitiveness. Trust it and have faith in it because it is there to help you.

When you have an intuition about someone, trust that it is right. If a white feather drifts past when you are thinking about a loved one who has passed and your intuition tells you that they are sending you a sign, trust that feeling. Have faith that it is a sign. You will feel a boost when you do because your spirit energy will link to the energy that is sending you the sign.

Kindness

If there is one short phrase that has been used more than any in the past few years it is this: "Be kind." It's almost become the motto of the times. How did we ever get to the stage when we need to be reminded to be decent to each other?

Around the world a series of events has sown division and distrust. Even if you are not political and don't follow the news, you can't ignore the fact that events such as the Brexit referendum and the election of Donald Trump as US President in 2016, and the coronavirus pandemic and the death of George Floyd in 2020, have created and revealed deep splits in society with people retreating into their tribes and judging others for their views and positions with no room for conversation. Social media has fanned the flames of these divisions, with its built-in algorithms that only serve up content to people that reinforces their views and biases, ensuring they live in echo chambers of like-minded people, never hearing alternative views in a constructive way.

Sadly, sometimes it takes big events to remind us of the good qualities we need to display, like the death of a popular public figure, or a tragedy. Who can forget the outpouring of grief after the death of Princess Diana, when the nation grieved together and sent so much love and compassion to her sons? More recently, for the social media generation, the tragic death of TV presenter Caroline Flack represented a watermark in which #BeKind became a theme (the hashtag was originally launched by Lucy Alexander in 2017 after her son took his life following years of being bullied). Caroline sadly took her own life after struggling with depression and anxiety. In one of her last Instagram posts she wrote, "In a world where you can be anything, be kind."

After her death, media outlets deleted recent online articles that had previously shamed and berated her, and in their place called for kindness. For fans it was a huge loss and as the calls for kindness grew louder, the effects rippled through the generations until even people who perhaps had never heard of her, let alone watched *Love Island*, heard the call and hopefully, as a consequence, reconsidered some of their actions. If they did, and if her death resulted in even a few people realising that if they were just a bit kinder the world would be a better place, then she left a fitting legacy.

Young people particularly can get drawn into some of the negative content and comments they see on social media, with its bullies and trolls and people spouting off angrily, and they can form the opinion that the world is a cruel and unkind place full of nasty people. This isn't the case and it's our job to let them know this.

Before social media, the world was full of nasty people. You just didn't hear them because they were in their own houses shouting at the walls. Whereas now, they can make their voices heard on Twitter or Instagram or TikTok. They are always going to be there and they're never going to change. And if they do, they'll be replaced by new nasty people. So, the best thing you can do is to get on with your life, live with kindness, be good to people and ignore them. Take this advice from an expert who has lived for decades with cynics and sceptics and people intent on ruining her reputation and livelihood.

Which brings me on to another aspect of behaviour that contributes to kindness, which is tolerance. In life we can be quick to judge and form negative opinions, whether that's judging people we don't know for the way they live and behave and the things they say, or judging people we do know. Try to show compassion and understanding. You don't have to like someone or agree with them in order to be tolerant. Even if you find them offensive, even if they themselves are not particularly nice, you can still be tolerant. It is very easy to react in a knee-jerk fashion to anything we don't agree with, and to immediately discount it, or take offence, even when no offence is meant.

Take the Black Lives Matter protests for example. For a lot of white people who had no experience of race issues, the knee-jerk refrain as soon as they heard the words "Black Lives Matter" was "All lives matter." They were not hearing the message as it was intended. Instead they were hearing "only *black* lives matter", which is offensive to those protesting and very obviously not the purpose of the movement. The best explanation I heard to help people understand the issues from a place of tolerance and compassion used the metaphor of a broken limb. All bones are important, but if you break your arm, you need the broken arm to be treated. That is the one that matters most and needs to take priority.

Trying to see things from another's perspective with compassion and without judgement is another key element of kindness and ties in closely with empathy, which is the ability to identify and understand another person's feelings, without experiencing them for yourself at that moment. It is the ability to be able to understand the world from another person's viewpoint; to walk in their shoes and to feel what it feels like to be that person.

Empathy allows your spirit energy to link with other people. It's like a magnetic force that draws you to people and helps you understand them. To be empathetic means being considerate to others. It is one of the most powerful tools a medium possesses and is a quality and a skill that I've always had, even as a little girl. Indeed, once I remember literally walking in another's shoes.

Let me explain. I had a difficult childhood. We were a very poor family and lived in a basement. There wasn't a lot to go around, but in the area we lived in there were always people worse off than we were. I was born in 1951 and the post-war years were tough for lots of families. Rationing was still in place when I was born and it was normal to see children dressed in hand-me-downs with holes in their school uniform and darned socks on their feet. Despite having very little, I would always offer to help someone worse off. At lunch I would give my food away if a classmate was hungry, and once, I took my shoes off to give to another girl at school when I realised hers were so worn that the soles of her feet were poking through the bottom of them. I still had a hole in my shoes, but I had a thick pad of newspaper in them to stop the cold getting through. I remember she took them gratefully, but the teacher shouted at me in class. She wasn't a particularly sympathetic woman. I put her shoes on and could feel the ground under my feet. I felt so sorry for that girl.

I'm not sure where that empathy came from, but I remember all the stories my mum used to tell me – because she used to speak to me like I was a 20-year-old rather than a seven-year-old – about the kids in the neighbourhood that didn't have anything, and the ones whose fathers had been killed in the war, or their houses had been bombed. I would cry at night when I thought about them and remember all those feelings and thoughts.

Throughout life that urge to help has stayed with me. I help charities and am a supporter and ambassador of the Pink Ribbon Foundation, having been involved with the charity for several years, using my live shows and social media platforms to raise awareness and money to support those affected by breast cancer. Even when I'm on tour I have got to know a number of the homeless people in the cities we visit and always help them out.

Perhaps it's easier to have empathy when you've endured hardships or had a problematic childhood.

Everyone can develop empathy. You just need to be a kind person connected to the other person's situation. We all have in us a capability to recognise, understand and connect with others because we all have spirit energy. It is the glue that binds us together.

Some people want to avoid empathy, perhaps because they feel powerless when faced with the suffering or plight of others, or they find it too upsetting to consider other people. Maybe it reminds them of unresolved traumas or sadness in their own lives. But empathy is not just about understanding suffering and trying to fix it. On a day-to-day scale, empathy is about understanding another person's perspective. We have the capability to recognise how that person sitting next to us on the train is feeling, trust me. And once you start to develop your spirit energy you don't even have to communicate, because with intuition you will be able to know.

But to begin with, aim for realistic kindness. None of us are saints after all and we can be forgiven for lapsing occasionally. It's part of being human, and as long as you recognise your shortcomings and be kind to yourself as well, you will be heading in the right direction.

As a final point about kindness and to end on a positive note, although sometimes the world can seem gloomy, particularly as we come out of the global pandemic and are facing so much change and uncertainty, it's important to remember that things do get better over time. We've already seen so much good, kindness and empathy during the past few years, which has opened the door to the possibility of a spiritual golden age.

And while there is sadly still a lot of hate and intolerance, history proves that attitudes do change. Look at homosexuality for example. When I was growing up, gay people had to hide their sexuality because they were persecuted. My uncle Tom was gay and could never tell his family, so he lived his personal life fearfully and in the shadows. I knew, of course, and so did my mother, but even when she gently suggested it to my dad he just laughed because he thought she was joking. To him, having a gay member of the family was a preposterous suggestion. Now, thankfully, the LGBTQ community is celebrated. It takes a society-wide effort to move the kindness agenda forward and we all have a part to play.

Positivity

When I was little, I had a shadow on my lung. It was so long ago now that I can't remember what caused it, but what I do remember is the nurse who came round every day to administer the injections I required over the course of a year to sort the problem out.

Let's just say bedside manner wasn't her forte. She'd turn up on a bicycle dressed like an extra from *Call the Midwife* and plonk me down roughly in a chair while my mum went to get a saucepan to boil water in, so the nurse could sterilise the needle. This was all done in our basement home, so you can imagine it had a certain gloomy medieval feel about it – dark, shadowy, boiling water, screaming child – you get the idea. This went on for months and forms one of my childhood memories.

We were latchkey kids. Another memory I have is of coming home to an empty house aged seven because the adults were working, getting the key from the hiding place in a hole in the wall (we didn't have anything to pinch even if burglars did get in) and lighting the fire because there was never any money in the meter and without a fire there would be no heat or light. I told my teacher this was part of my after-school routine one day and she didn't bat an eyelid.

Imagine saying that to a teacher today. Social services would be round your house quicker than you could say "care order".

On Sunday, my mum would get the newspapers and once Mum and Dad had read them, me and my sister would carefully cut the paper into strips and my dad would string it all together, and that would be our toilet paper for the week. In honesty it was better than the horrible slippery stuff that you got at school. I don't think I experienced the luxury of soft toilet tissue until I was in my early teens.

The funny thing is, I can never remember feeling really sad, or depressed. I was an upbeat child and looked forward to life.

Meanwhile, today there is an epidemic of anxiety and depression amongst young people. And I can understand this because they have different problems. They are growing up in a world where their futures are unsure, where housing is unaffordable and where climate change is a looming disaster. I think given the choice I'd rather have grown up when I did. Despite the hardships that were endured by children of my generation, we didn't have the same levels of anxiety and depression.

The reason for this was two-fold. Firstly, you were neither allowed to nor had time to dwell on your problems, and secondly, and most importantly, you were brought up to be positive. You accepted what you had with gratitude and hoped for a better future. You were taught to face adversity with stoicism and a stiff upper lip and told that if you worked hard, you would do alright. You looked on the bright side.

Positivity is another key to spirit energy, because a positive mindset gives you the ability to see life from an upbeat perspective. In all the readings I've done, the strongest energies I've felt are from happy, positive people. I think this is because positivity is the antidote to negativity, which repels spirit energy. Negativity leads to fear and doubt. People who doubt have no faith or trust.

The six keys to unlock your spirit power

We will all suffer at one time or another. What determines how that affects you is how you deal with it. If you are the type of person who meets negative with negative, you will attract negativity. We all know people who bring the atmosphere of a room down and who seem to suck the joy from a situation. These people have chosen to side with negativity. Their energy is negatively charged.

My glass is always half full. It is a hard mindset to maintain sometimes and I have been through tough situations, but I have looked at my work and tried to take positives from it. Sometimes you must meet misfortune and accept that it was meant to be and if you cannot do anything to change it, then move forward positively in the best way you can.

Another element that I link to positivity is forgiveness, because you can't forgive someone unless you feel some form of positivity towards them. This is a hard one for me because while I know I am capable of forgiveness, there are hypothetical situations in which I'm not sure I could forgive someone, and I guess this is what differentiates the saints among us from those who are just trying to live a more spiritual life. If somebody murdered someone close to me for example, I don't know how I'd forgive.

I saw a report recently in which a woman whose 13-year-old son was stabbed to death was explaining that she forgave his killers. If I was in her situation, I'd want to wring their necks, and I know deep down inside that's not spiritual, but that's what I'd want to do. I'd also want to die, which isn't a positive outlook. The mother was seeing the situation from an incredibly empathetic viewpoint. She explained that the killers were from deprived backgrounds and broken homes and that it was a social issue, which I can understand, but I also know that killing is fundamentally wrong and that many people come from deprived backgrounds but manage to overcome their challenges without killing others.

If we blame evil behaviour on social circumstances, or bad parenting, are we just kicking the can down the road? From a spiritual viewpoint, these thoughts and my difficulty in overcoming what would be a need for justice and revenge show my limitations. Taking a life is forbidden. It's one of the worst actions one person can do to another. Anyone who murders has bad in them but there are killings that happen without intent. There are people who have killed for reasons they believe are just. Look at soldiers. Are they deserving of forgiveness if they kill an enemy combatant? I believe they are. Or if someone is punched in a fight, falls, hits their head and dies. Is their killer morally any more deserving of forgiveness than someone who murders to satisfy a blood lust?

Forgiveness is a theme that comes up repeatedly in my work, because it is associated with guilt, one of the primary emotions that people feel after the death of a loved one. Did we do enough for them, were we there for them, did we love them enough? Because we feel guilty, we often seek forgiveness.

Sometimes spirits who have done bad things on Earth feel the need to come back to ask for forgiveness from their loved ones. Why is this? I have a feeling it is to redress the balance between good and bad and to cleanse their spirit energy, which is tainted by the bad things they did. Perhaps they get sent back to make amends.

One memorable example of this happened during one of my shows at a theatre in the Home Counties.

I picked up the energy of a man in spirit who I knew had served a very long prison sentence before his death. The energy did not feel as positive and pure as most and I've learned over the years that in those cases, the person connected to that energy has usually done something particularly bad in life. We all do bad things of course, but the good will outweigh the bad and our energy passes over with a balanced symmetry.

The messages that came through from this man's energy were names: Michael and Margaret. I told the audience what I was picking up and also explained that I had a bad feeling about what I was receiving.

A woman in the audience stood and explained that her brother, Michael, died from a blow to the back of the head and her mother, Margaret, died from a brain tumour.

"You haven't got a link to someone who did something really bad have you?" I asked.

She told me her father served a 25-year prison sentence.

Usually when someone takes a message and a connection is made, I get more information from spirit. It's like a phone connection being established and I'm the telephone exchange. I realised the man had died in prison. His daughter confirmed this.

I sensed that spirit wanted to repent.

The reading got even more shocking. I sensed a girl and the name Sarah. The woman nodded sadly and said she was Sarah's godmother.

"It's another tragic tale," she said. "I saw you a few years ago and you came through with a message from Sarah. You said she was locked in a van. I didn't take the message that time. I was too scared."

To gasps from the audience, she then confirmed that her goddaughter Sarah had been abducted and murdered and her body had been found in woods. Her remains had been eaten by foxes.

The six keys to unlock your spirit power

I couldn't imagine what a tough life that lady had, having faced such family tragedy, but she was willing to forgive her father for the crimes he committed and in doing so, I could feel the goodness in her energy. In the face of all she had endured, she was moving on from the past with peace and positivity, and even though she didn't realise it, this made her a very spiritual person.

Purpose

Everyone needs a purpose in life. When you have a purpose, you have direction. It doesn't have to be some grand purpose leading to a lifelong achievement. Your purpose could be raising your children, which is a vital and noble purpose. It could be looking after your parents or getting a promotion.

But we also need a small-scale everyday purpose in order to get on with life, because spirit energy is like any other form of energy: when it's excited, switched on or stimulated, it gets more powerful. Purpose makes us do things; it stops lethargy and promotes positivity because it provides us with a goal and a reason to live.

I find purpose in many things, like when I do my daily guidance online for example and I get people telling me that I've given them a reason to be positive for the day. My purpose is to always be able to get up and go to work.

If people say I can never find a purpose, I answer, make your purpose for today to be happy.

Have a purpose every day and you'll discover that it gives you motivation and energy. We all have down days when we are ill or don't feel right or just can't be bothered. A purpose lifts you out of the rut, it motivates and nourishes. It gives your energy a boost and wants you to be alive and positively active.

Spirit energy reacts to spiritual purpose, not materialist purpose. So, if you make your purpose to buy yourself a new car, that's not going to earn you much spiritual capital. You might be putting money in the bank, but you're not collecting any spiritual Clubcard points. That is a common mistake people make. They aim for material things in the hope they will achieve happiness, but we all know what happens. You get the money and you buy the car, or the handbag, or the shoes, then, within a few months you want something else. Satisfaction comes from more meaningful achievements.

Don't judge yourself harshly if this is you because we all fall into this trap. I'm really trying to practise what I preach in my 70th year and attempting to buy less because I'm a sucker for a lovely piece of clothing, or a new pair of shoes. But now just being able to look myself in the face and say, you know what, you were happy today and you didn't go out and you didn't buy anything, to me, that's achieving a purpose.

There are also inner purposes that we pursue. By reading this book, your purpose is to unlock your spirit energy and nurture it, which will lead to self-improvement. My purpose in writing this book is to encourage you to investigate your spirit and to help you on your spiritual path.

Being spiritual also gives us a purpose, and in turn it allows us to focus on and harness our energy, which in turn boosts it.

I know that my purpose isn't to convince others that there is life after death, or that spirits from the afterlife can connect with us. I'm not here to change anyone's mind. I'm not out to convert. Definitely not. That's too big a responsibility. I leave people to come to their own conclusions about what I do and, in many ways, I'm still coming to my own acceptance of my work, which might surprise you. But daily I scrutinise what I'm doing. I believe and I have faith, but I don't have all the answers and I constantly ask questions of myself.

In the afterlife our spirit energy has a purpose too, which is perhaps why we need purpose when we are alive. The spirit energy that I connect with when I do readings is here to help those it connects with. It can warn of problems and danger or help with our grief by giving validation of an afterlife. It can also help us come to terms with our own mortality and to give us reassurance that life does go on.

Authenticity

I've previously written about honesty, and the importance of being honest with yourself and others. This ties in with the theme of authenticity, which also includes truthfulness and openness.

Authenticity is the ability to be your honest self, to say what you honestly think in a kind and compassionate way and to do what feels right, not what you think is expected of you. Authentic people are genuine people and they tell the truth. Spirit energy reacts to authenticity and honesty.

There have been countless times during my career when I've received a message that I have felt might be perceived as offensive or weird by the audience, or the person I'm reading for, but I have to be authentic and truthful in what I'm receiving and to pass the message on as I am receiving it, because it's given to me in the way I receive it for a reason. And 99 per cent of the time the process works. The message, no matter how weird or random, means something to the person it is meant for.

As an example, I recently did a reading for a woman. She was in her fifties and the reading was done via video as it took place during the pandemic. She was a pretty lady with long straight blonde hair and a strong South London accent. Even before we'd established a bit of easy chit-chat, I could feel a spirit knocking at the door, so to speak. It's a hard feeling to describe but it starts with random flashes in my mind, like thoughts dropping into my brain. How do I know it's not my brain making its own thoughts, you might ask. Because the thoughts do not relate to me, and have nothing to do with my life; they feel alien, and they are not spoken with my internal dialogue. The best way I can describe it is like when you've slept in a funny position and you wake up and you can't feel your arm, it feels like it belongs to someone else. That's what the psychic part of my brain goes like.

Anyway, I could feel there was a spirit (it felt like a man) anxious to make contact with this lady. I explained to the lady that I had a man in spirit who was very eager to connect with her. She smiled and nodded, as if she was expecting someone. Once a message is 'taken', which means acknowledged, the process starts in earnest. It's that telephone connection where the speaker and the receiver are linked. Most of the time the first things that pop into my mind are names. That makes perfect sense.

When we answer a call, we ask who's calling (or we did in the days before caller ID). The name I got was Rod. I relayed this to the woman and tears sprung in her eyes. They were tears of happiness and she nodded.

"That's my dad," she smiled. "Rodney."

I sensed that Rod was a bit of a character. A bit of a joker.

"He was a right one, your dad, wasn't he," I said. "He's laughing, he thinks it's hilarious that you've gone to see a psychic."

She laughed too.

"He always thought it was a load of rubbish," she said.

"He doesn't now," I giggled.

And then the strangest word popped into my mind. It was so random that had I not had the benefit of decades of experience I might well have ignored it, for fear of showing myself up. But authenticity and honesty are vital, so I said it.

"He's saying the word 'celery'," I frowned. "In fact, he's not just saying it he's singing it. Does that mean anything to you? Did he particularly like celery?"

For one terrible minute I wondered if he'd died choking on a piece of celery. He hadn't though. I found out later that he'd died of Covid.

The woman started laughing.

"Oh my God," she exclaimed. "It's a football chant. He was a lifelong Chelsea fan and never missed a home game. When I was young he used to take me. There was a chant about celery and he used to cover my ears whenever the fans sung it. I asked him why and he never told me until I was much older and heard the full version."

Well, that blew my mind. It was so specific that it left us in no doubt about the message. There was no way I could have known any of that and the father offered it because he knew it would validate his presence. That's why as a medium, authenticity is so important. I know that spirit energy is drawn to honest people. It's why I don't dress my practice up with any flourishes like I know some mediums do.

I'm not mocking anybody, or judging, but I do struggle to understand sometimes why some mediums will affect a spooky voice and weird mannerisms when they are giving readings. It doesn't affect the strength of the energy you are tapping in to. It is so common some people expect it and are surprised when they meet me and I'm just normal Sally from Surrey, with a normal office and without a headscarf. When I used to see people at home some would come in and ask whether they needed to be barefoot in order to be grounded.

"Please yourself," I'd laugh. "Whatever floats your boat."

I had one male client who always used to come dressed from head to foot in white linen and would sit cross-legged in the chair. He always looked uncomfortable.

"It doesn't change what I'm going to see," I'd tell him. "But if you are happier with that, then that's fine by me."

Maybe he saw something on television and thought that's how you're supposed to act in real life.

I did an evening of clairvoyance many years ago for the National Psychic Association in London. They were lovely people and it was an honour to be asked there. When I arrived and walked in, the person who met me explained that they had a room ready for me to prepare in. They showed me to this lovely room full of candles and drapes and explained that they were going to leave me for as long as I needed to meditate and get attuned.

"It's fine," I said. "But I'd love a cup of tea."

They seemed puzzled. "But how do you prepare?" they asked.

"I don't. I just walk on."

They were quite surprised. Maybe some people do need an hour to meditate and sit there in a room full of candles but that's never been the way I work and if I started to behave in that way, I think my work would suffer because somehow it would cause interference in my energy flow.

Openness is one of the key elements that boosts spirit energy. If you are not open to spirit you will never see the wonders it offers.

There will always be people who think we do not have souls and that we do not possess spirit energy. There will always be doubt. You might be surprised to know that I welcome that. I think it is a good thing because it makes us ask questions. But just because you have doubts about something, doesn't mean it doesn't exist. Doubt doesn't mean you should discount something altogether just because you don't understand it. This is where the sceptics get it wrong. They dismiss it out of hand. We can't see atoms and sub-atomic particles but we know they are there. At the end of the day, when it comes to psychic events and messages from the dead, something is happening and I am proof of that.

Some of the people who come to my shows have doubts and I am privileged that I can answer them with solid validation and send them away with a more open, accepting mind. For example, at one show, I kept seeing a St Christopher on a gold chain. I couldn't quite work out which message it related to because it was a busy night and there were so many messages that were interlinked.

Finally, a lady stood to take it.

"I put a St Christopher on this evening because I was hoping my dad might come through. I've never worn it before," she said. She was doubtful the pendant would work, but she was open to the possibility that maybe her father would show himself.

A name popped into my mind.

"Was your father called Gordon?" I asked.

"No… that was his brother. He's in spirit."

"And is there the name Duncan?"

"That was his other brother," she confirmed. "I didn't believe this before I came." She was nothing if not honest.

I told her that it was okay to have doubts. I still do, because sometimes what happens to me seems so mad.

"I still struggle with knowing what I do," I told her. "Yet it happens. All I know is I see, touch, smell and taste spirit and I get things in my head."

It is usually men who doubt. At a show in Australia, a man was with his wife in the audience and I picked him out because there was a spirit coming through to me who wanted to give him a message. He was a big man, a proper Aussie bloke, and he raised a quizzical eyebrow when I pointed him out. He was totally sceptical. His father was in spirit and I got his name, then his father told me the nickname he was called when he was younger. I could see the doubt peel away from this man as he stood and listened to the detail I was giving him. He started to well up.

After the show, he came up to me as I was signing books and he was a changed man. He explained that he had arrived that evening as a sceptic but was leaving with belief and that he had undergone a life-changing experience.

All of which illustrates that if you are prepared to open your mind up to the possibility, you might be amazed what you find. If you remain closed, if you are not honest with yourself or others, you may never achieve what you are truly capable of.

Even sceptics can be persuaded and it's never too late to overcome cynicism. I have had hundreds of sceptics who've come through to me from the afterlife. On one memorable occasion, a man's three daughters were in the audience. He was a total non-believer throughout his life, but he came through with his message loud and clear and there was a huge amount of energy radiating from him as he connected with his children. They told me that all through his life, whenever he heard about mediums, he would scoff and discount them as charlatans. Nevertheless, when it came to the opportunity, he was the first to come through and make contact, even though there were other relatives in spirit of the girls waiting to connect. He barged his way to the front of the queue! I smile when I think what a very pleasant surprise it would have been for him when he passed and realised death was just the beginning.

He found his truth in death, but with honesty, authenticity and openness we can find ours in life.

Being present

Which brings me on to the final of the six keys that unlock your spirit energy and start you on your way to building up your spiritual capital. And that is to cherish the present. Not the one you get at Christmas or birthdays, the one you are in now. In other words, as much as you can, live in the moment. Don't live in the past, don't dwell too much on past mistakes. Make your peace and move on. And don't place so much attention on the future that you forget to live today.

There's one really simple key idea here that we all overlook. How we live in the present decides how good or bad our lives are, because we don't live in the past or the future. Imagine your life as a long fuse, like those ones in the old movies. You are the flame moving along that fuse. The past is ash, the future is there, but yet to be. All the energy and all the life is there in the present, in that flame burning along to its predetermined end.

The six keys to unlock your spirit power

One of the fundamental mistakes people make when they commit to living a more spiritual life, is that they concentrate so much energy on cleansing the past and creating a better future that they don't live in the now. Some people get so serious they forget to have fun and put their own pleasure aside, assuming that once they have achieved their idea of spirituality, they'll experience pleasure then. Blimey! Enjoy life. That's what it's there for. You shouldn't aspire to be a clean-living, virtuous angel. I'm not preaching hedonism and wild abandon, but it really doesn't do anyone any harm to live a little now and then. In fact, it's good for the soul.

I don't have a halo over my head and I'm honest enough with myself to know I never will. Being virtuous is exhausting. It's fine to have a drink now and then, or pig out. As long as you don't overdo it all the time.

If you fail at something, learn from your mistakes and move on. Don't keep going back and beating yourself up about things that happened in the past that you can't change. If you've hurt someone, make good and move on.

If you continually rake over mistakes and fixate on detoxing your mind every single day, you're not going to have a life in the present. It's a bit like going to a spa every day. You can only do so much before it becomes ineffectual. Some people can get so preoccupied with planning for the future and trying to live a healthy life, both physically and spiritually, that they end up frightened of living. What they're actually doing is narrowing their life and their opportunities to experience things in the present.

Take the chances to do new and exciting things when you can and don't worry too much about the future, because it will arrive no matter what.

Embrace life.

Chapter 7

The love connection

There's one human emotion above all the others that feeds spirit energy, and that's love. Love is like a multi-tool: it holds people together, it's the fuel that feeds energy and it's the pump that makes sure energy continues to flow through life and in death. Love is what ensures that whenever I do a reading for an individual or an audience, the energy connection always hits its target.

In a simple way, love lights up a person's energy which allows another person's energy, living or dead, to find it and lock in on it. When we love others, our energies link and when we love each other, over time, our energies intertwine. For people who have loved each other for a long time, their energies almost become one, to the extent that when one dies, their energies are still linked across the divide between the Earth plane and the next dimension. We also have that special energy link with our children. I think that perhaps when we have children we pass on a part of our spirit energy to them, in the same way we pass on our DNA. It's a permanent link that lasts forever.

This love link was powerfully evident in the case of a man I met several years ago and who came to me in his dying years because he wanted answers to a specific question.

The gentleman was in his eighties and had been diagnosed with a terminal disease. He knew his time was short and when he sat down in front of me, I could sense that he carried grief with him. I felt the presence of a very young boy and in my mind's eye I saw a river and felt panic and then cold. I shivered.

"You lost a son when he was very young," I said to the man. "He drowned?"

The man nodded and explained that his little boy was four and had drowned in a river when they had been on a family boating trip.

"Is he okay?" the man asked.

"Yes, he is," I smiled, "he's here with you, he's always been with you."

It was true: the link formed by the love between father and son had remained unbroken by the son's death. The love had kept the son's energy connected to his father's and the old man had felt his son's presence throughout his life.

I picked up more.

"When your wife died, your boy was there with her," I explained. "And he watches over you too."

I felt a pain in my chest and understood the meaning.

"You had heart problems," I said.

The man explained that yes, he'd suffered a mild heart attack several years before.

"He was there, in the hospital, looking over you," I explained.

"I know. I felt him," sobbed the man.

And then I saw one of those random images in my mind that are so peculiar that they can only mean something very specific. I saw a box of dusty old toys in a shed.

"You couldn't throw the toys away, could you? You go to the shed and you hold them. That's when he feels you the most," I explained.

Nearly every day, that poor man would go into his shed, pick up those toys and cry for his lost son.

I knew then why he'd come to see me. He was in the winter of his years, facing death, and he almost felt guilty that he'd lived so long when his son had died so early. All he wanted then was to be with his son.

"I want to be with him," he said quietly. "Will he be there?"

I could have wept myself.

"Of course," I told him. "He'll be there with his mum. You'll be together again in a place surrounded by love."

Later he showed me a photograph of a little boy with a mop of blond hair and a cheeky smile. He explained that he had slipped, fallen into the river and drowned. For the rest of his life the man had carried the love he had for his son and it had never diminished.

When you understand how deeply love connects, you can start to see how people die of broken hearts. When two people are so tightly linked together, when the energy of one passes over, perhaps the energy of the survivor decides to go with it. Maybe the pull to the other side is too strong and your energy just says, I'm off.

It happened to the grandparents of a close relative of mine. His granddad and gran had been married for 60 years and were devoted to each other. The gran, let's call her Joan, got ill and ended up in a nursing home and then a hospital. Her husband, we'll call Jack, was distraught. He visited her every day and struggled to live without her by his side, as she had been for most of his life.

He watched as his beloved wife's condition deteriorated and would spend hours by her side, holding her hand, talking about their life together as she slipped in and out of consciousness in the last days of her life. He knew her life was ebbing away and wanted to be with her every second he could, but he was old and frail too and each evening his son had to persuade him to go home so he could sleep and be rested for the following day. The energy between the couple would have been so intense in those last days.

Each night before he left, he kissed her and told her he loved her. She loved him too, and she didn't want to put him through the pain and agony of being there when she died. She passed away peacefully early one morning while he was a few miles away at home, getting ready to go and see her.

The home called his son who decided that it would be best to tell his father in person, so he could be there to comfort him, rather than tell him over the phone. The son drove to his father's house, steeled himself to deliver the news and let himself in with the keys he had. He opened the door and called to his dad to let him know he was there. He walked through the door and gasped. His dad was lying on the floor in the hall. He was dead.

An ambulance was called, but the paramedics knew straight away that there was nothing they could do. Jack had been dead for a couple of hours, they explained. It appeared to have happened quite suddenly.

When the family pieced together the last hours of Jack's life, they realised that he would have got home from seeing his wife the previous evening, had something to eat, gone to bed, risen in the morning, got dressed and then collapsed and died soon after Joan had died. There was no way he could have known.

I've heard hundreds of stories like this from people I've met over the years. They are examples of people dying of broken hearts. But Jack didn't know his wife was dead, so how do you describe his sudden passing?

Easy. Jack and Joan were inseparable. Their lives and their energy were intrinsically linked. They were from a generation that was not prone to mawkish displays of emotion. They grew up in the war and when hardship hit, they just got on with it. But after so many years together, they both knew they couldn't live without the other and had an intuitive link that they wouldn't have been consciously aware of. When Joan died, Jack knew instinctively, because his energy would have felt it. And his energy was so tightly linked to Joan's, that when hers left her body, his left his.

Some people I tell this story to respond by saying how sad it is. But is it? Of course, it's always sad for those left behind, but for Jack and Joan it's not sad at all. Neither of them could have lived without the other. Jack's life without his beloved wife would have been miserable.

The love connection

Love is an umbilical cord. It links you to your partner, your husband, your wife, your parents and your kids. It is lovely and comforting to know that when you die you are still attached to those people and every time one of them thinks of you their spirit energy runs along that cord and touches yours.

We keep that love alive with memories and in return those who have passed thank us with the signs they send.

*   *   *

I often get asked what happens if somebody hasn't got anyone they love. What if they've had no kids or haven't been married or had no partner? Firstly, it's very rare that someone has never loved or been loved by anyone, but admittedly there are such people. They are not alone, however, because we all have parents and ancestors and they will be there, their energy will be attached to ours, even if we never knew them in life.

The way love interacts with energy is so complex that I don't have all the answers, but I do know that the two are almost interchangeable. Love is an energy and spirit energy thrives with love.

Those six keys to unlock your spirit energy that I described in the previous chapter are all linked to love in some way or another. Having faith comes with love, kindness is a loving behaviour, positive people are loving people, in order to have a purpose you need to love your goals, real love is authentic and being present for someone shows you love them. If you practise these elements you will live a more loving life, which will nourish your spirit energy and build your spiritual capital.

Love allows energy to manifest unseen in all sorts of places. We don't know it, but we project love into the souvenirs and mementos we collect through life. It sits there, unseen in the photographs and personal items that we hold and that belong to the people we love. When those people pass, those items hold that energy. Think of it like evidence in a TV crime drama. You can't see it with the naked eye, but when you shine a special light over it, it lights up.

As a medium I am particularly sensitive to this kind of psychic detective work and will often ask people I do readings for to bring emotive objects with them, because those items hold energy that I can tap into and read.

Energy doesn't just manifest in items, it permeates buildings and spaces. It stays in the walls of homes and, in the case of some hauntings, replays the same scene from former lives like a DVD that keeps skipping back to the same point. In that way a spirit becomes a parasite. It can attach itself.

The love connection

Most of us go through life without ever feeling or noticing it, which is why I wanted to share these stories and techniques with you, to help open people up to the possibilities of living a more spiritual life. When you boost your spirit energy and become more attuned to the spirit energy of others, you will notice that other world much more. Your eyes will be opened.

Like me, you'll walk into buildings and be able to feel their energies. You might even be able to identify the individual energies manifesting inside them.

It's been one of the constant aspects of my life that whenever I move, there's always a ghost in the house I buy. I think I am drawn to them. Most recently, when viewing a property, I walked into the kitchen and I saw a man in spirit standing by the kitchen sink. Then upstairs I saw a woman. They obviously didn't get on in life because they had chosen to stay in different parts of the house. Both were very pronounced in my perception, but no one else saw them, which is often the case. Spirits will only usually show their energies for specific people, but we all have spirits around us all the time. It's like an unseen mist as we walk through life, or a gentle breeze that touches your cheek periodically.

Some of us recognise an ever-present energy, like a guiding spirit or a guardian angel. We feel it in times of need and we draw strength from it. Some of us can identify the person that energy belonged to. Inevitably it will be someone we loved and who loved us. I always refer to mine as my granddad and I know he's there, watching over me. But often that presence I feel are my other family spirits around me.

Even the biggest cynics, when pushed, will admit to feeling things that they can't explain. This is because sceptics are no different from anyone else in that they feel love and have loved ones; therefore they have energy links and energy is an irrepressible force that manages to break through the strongest barriers. They know that there are forces around them that they can't explain, they just don't want to admit it.

We need love in our lives almost as much as we need food and water. Love feeds our energy and without it, we wither. Love is strongest with contact, which is why there were so many tragic stories about people forced into isolation during the pandemic. And so much loneliness suffered by people who lived on their own and were unable to connect to their friends and family due to lockdown. In those cases the invisible links of love were as important to those people as the FaceTime and Zoom calls that allowed them to keep a window open into the lives of their families.

Some of the hardest readings I've been asked to do in the past two years have involved families whose loved ones died while in isolation, or in care homes, where sons and daughters were unable to be with their parents in their dying hours.

The predominant feeling in these instances is of guilt. Children feel an unreasonable sense of guilt that they were unable to help in the dying hours of their parents' lives.

In one such reading, which due to restrictions I hosted via video, a woman wanted closure after her father had died suddenly having been admitted to a Covid ward. She had been working from home and couldn't get to him before the ambulance came and took him away. She'd been stressed when he called her, spluttering and out of breath, to say that he had called 999 because he was struggling to breathe. She told me that she'd asked him if he really was that bad because hospitals were filling up and every bed was vital.

She felt so guilty about making that off-the-cuff remark, and of having the slightest doubt that her father was gravely ill because she had not been able to visit him to see for herself.

"He got admitted in the afternoon and he died overnight," she cried. "I never had the chance to say goodbye or to say sorry."

But her father's spirit had been with her all the time, and I could feel a desperate need from it to soothe her and to let her know that there was nothing to be sorry about.

"He knows you feel terrible about that last call," I told her. "He needs you to know that you have nothing to feel guilty about. He is so proud of you, and he wants you know that he's at peace and will always be in your heart."

The reading contained other pieces of information that left no doubt in the daughter's mind that her father was with her, and when we said our goodbyes she was in a much more peaceful and accepting place. I could feel the peace in her father's energy, too.

Those of us with loving families are lucky. There are plenty of people who can't stand their family and who are estranged from loved ones. There's an old saying, you can choose your friends but you can't choose your family, and it's very apt. I'm lucky, I have family I love and who love me, but I also have a group of special people I call my chosen family. We can all have these: they are our closest friends. The ones that we know will have our back through thick and thin and who will always be there for us. The luckiest among us have real family *and* chosen family. We've all had to rely on each other these last few years and for those without blood family, chosen families have been a lifeline. Bonds will have been made in the pandemic that will last a lifetime and there have been literally billions of outpourings of love and support across the globe that have helped create this new age of spiritual energy.

The love between chosen family is just as strong as the love between blood family in many cases. We all have people we call brother from another mother, or sister from another mister! They are there when we need them, we trust them with our lives, they are compassionate and kind, and also honest with us, because honesty is really important in any relationship. Often our chosen families are the ones we turn to for advice about our real family, and the ones we tell the things we couldn't tell our mums and dads or brothers and sisters.

Lots of you will have lost loved ones to Covid and problems relating to the pandemic, and your chosen family will be there to support you through that and to almost make up, in some way or another, for that loss.

Humans have a need to know that there are people there for us. We need to be part of a group. This is a primal instinct driven by our desire to love and be loved.

This need for connection and to build a chosen family can in some cases be helped by social media. It is where social media can come into its own. It gets a lot of bad press, but when you look at platforms like Facebook and

Instagram there is no denying that they have made it easier than ever to make connections with other people.

Detractors will say that Facebook friends aren't real friends. I would argue that they are, and that millions of true friendships, as rich as any offline, have been built and sustained through social media. It acts to alleviate the boundaries of geography. It can build communities.

You can certainly make real friends on Facebook and other sites, in the same way my generation made penfriends when we were younger. We never looked at them as inferior to other friends, they were just a different type of friend.

Used in the correct way, in a loving, realistic and responsible way, our online friends can certainly get us through tough times. In fact, social media provides a whole new way of being able to connect to people we can relate to. Sometimes it's easier to talk to people online than it is to talk to people face-to-face. By all means be wary of the negative side of social media, but remember that it has many positive sides too, both in terms of friendship and of course in terms of romantic love. It is probably more common now to meet a romantic partner online than it is to meet in person; during the pandemic and lockdown, cyberspace was full of love, because that was the only place to meet someone.

The love connection

Spirituality makes you attractive and there is no doubt that attraction develops easily between people who are spiritually attuned. We have an innate ability to recognise others who are on the same spiritual wavelength as we are, and even if we are not as developed spiritually as some, if we practise the six elements, our character and personality will be attractive to others.

It is always very easy to spot an open, positive and kind person. They radiate good vibes, which of course is their spirit energy, and our senses are designed to identify these vibes and lock on to the positive ones that belong to people who are approachable and kind.

Indeed, our spirit energy will often be there, in the background, without us even being aware, guiding us to make choices in love. The stronger our energy, and the better we are at identifying spiritual people, the better those choices will be.

Our spirit energy feeds on love, so wants us to have as much love in our lives as we possibly can. And for that reason, it will often show us the way when it comes to matters of the heart. Humans have known this for hundreds of years, assigning those sudden feelings and hunches we get about prospective partners to arrows from Cupid's bow.

Love intuition has been represented as being controlled by otherworldly beings such as Eros or

Aphrodite, the God and Goddess of love. Although we choose who we fall in love with based on a whole host of conscious and subconscious decisions and information, there is definitely a spiritual element, especially when couples meet by chance. People who are meant to be together are brought together by spirit energy.

We can even be helped along by the energy of those around us in spirit, when they provide signs and pointers when it comes to finding love. The secret here is to learn to listen to what they are saying. And that means following your intuition rather than your head.

First impressions are very powerful and often they prove right, because we make snap judgements about people we meet based on a whole host of unconscious clues. Those first impressions are unclouded by conscious information and are often spot on. They are informed by our intuition and our intuition feeds our spirit energy.

It is all about trust. If we trust and know they are there, they will help us. Spirit doesn't want us to be lonely. It wants to enrich our lives.

You should also never be afraid to ask spirit for a sign and for guidance. It will answer. If you have lost a loved one and have moved on in your grief to the point where you are ready to start another relationship, but are worried that you will upset the person you lost, ask

The love connection

for guidance. I have never yet come across a spirit who was not pleased when a loved one moved on and found love again. Jealousy does not exist in the afterlife. If our instinct tells us it is the right thing to do, we should listen because that's our spirit energy guiding us.

Love works differently on the Earth plane than in the afterlife when it comes to our intimate relationships. Here, the love we have with our boyfriends, girlfriends, husbands and wives is exclusive. On the whole we have one partner at a time and it is common to settle down with just one person. Monogamy is the general rule unless you are unfaithful or a swinger! I am devoted to John and he is devoted to me and that excludes all others. It is a lovely way to be and for most people that arrangement feels right.

In spirit, however, love is inclusive. Everyone is drawn into each other's loving energy. Don't get the wrong idea. There is nothing seedy about it. The love that binds spirit energy is a pure love while flesh and blood comes with certain urges and needs.

In the vast majority of cases, where a spirit has come through and registered that a widow or widower has moved on with a new lover, the energy is accepting and encouraging.

169

Secret Spirit

* * *

One of the most common subjects that I am consulted on when I read for others is love. Will I find it, Sally? Is he or she the right person for me? Are they cheating on me? It usually starts with a conversation about something else but always ends up focused on love. And that's perfectly understandable, because for humans, love is life, it is our soul fuel. That's why losing love is so hard. It's like running out of petrol.

You will no doubt find that as you develop your spirit energy and grow your spiritual capital, those around you will rely on you for advice, particularly about love.

These conversations require empathy, honesty, authenticity and often courage to sometimes tell people things they don't want to hear.

I've had countless examples of people who come to me and I know that their relationship with their partner is dead and gone. The best way I can help them is to tell them the truth, so they can move on. Most already know, but they just need the confirmation. Sadly, tough love is what's required in those situations. The truth doesn't always make it any easier, because in many cases the person still doesn't accept it. Like the saying goes, the truth hurts. And sometimes it is much easier not to tell the truth, but in so doing we lose our authenticity.

The love connection

Often during readings it's not even me that gives the dire prognosis and reads the last rites to a dying relationship, it's the person in spirit connected to the receiver. Over the years, I've had to tell countless people that their relatives in spirit are advising them to ditch a boyfriend or girlfriend, or to get a divorce. Imagine that. It's one thing hearing it from a spiritual advisor, but another hearing it from your dead mother.

I'm always finding myself in awkward situations where I'm presented with a message that I know isn't what the receiver necessarily wants to hear. Nevertheless I have to have faith that the information is being given for a reason and I know that when spirits give advice on earthly relations to their loved ones, they do so out of love. They want us to be happy and if that means suffering the short-term pain of a broken relationship in exchange for the freedom to find a more meaningful love, then we need to listen and trust their advice.

Chapter 8

Learning about loss

I'm starting this chapter off with a disclaimer: I cannot make loss any less painful.

When you lose a loved one, no one can say anything that makes it easier. I've done thousands of readings for grieving relatives where I've been able to pass on messages from their lost loved ones. These give them validation that their loved ones are at peace, and hope that they will see them again in the afterlife. Even my intervention, however, does not make their grief any easier.

For most of us, the hardest thing we'll ever endure in our lives is loss and the worst kind of loss is the loss of a loved one.

Grief is a symptom of loss. It is psychological, but it can be so intense that it leads to pain and in some cases even death. At its worst it is a raw, visceral, emotional pain that comes in waves and often overwhelms, leaving the sufferer incapable of thinking straight or functioning. In my experience, it opens hearts to feelings that many people have never endured before and for that reason it can be shocking, shattering lives and knocking the bereaved for six. It is horrendous and in extreme cases, those suffering from grief will sometimes wish they were the person who died because death seems to be an easier proposition than the grief of being left behind.

Most of us will experience grief in some form in our lifetimes. The only people who never experience it are those who die young. But when they die, the grief that their relatives experience is one of the worst kinds of grief. It is mixed with helplessness, anger and deep feelings of injustice.

Grief isn't always about the death of a person. We can grieve over any kind of loss, depending on the value to us of that which is lost, or the way in which it was lost. People commonly grieve over the loss of pets, because they are a part of the family. And they can also grieve over the loss of a possession, or something within their life, depending on the amount of spirit energy they've invested into it.

For example, back in the eighties, when I had a young family and before I had found fame as a medium, John and I went into partnership with someone and set up a business. We were working hard trying to better our lives and went on holiday with the kids one summer. When we came back we discovered that while we were away thousands of pounds had been taken out of the business, and when we looked further, we discovered a trail of questionable transactions. As a result, we not only lost the business, we also had to move.

John loved the house we were in, but we could no longer afford the mortgage and had to downsize. The incident hit him really hard. He struggled not only to come to terms with losing the house, but he also lost his job and income and he struggled with the way in which the loss occurred. Someone had done us over and, as the supposed provider and protector, John felt angry and frustrated. His pride was battered. He felt genuine grief which lasted for five years. We couldn't even drive past our old house because it upset him too much and brought back bad memories.

People tend to assign levels to grief. I'm sure there will be a few of you reading this and thinking, "The loss of a house and a job isn't as bad as losing a parent, or a dog." But grief is unique to the person who experiences it. Who are we to judge the losses of others? Grief requires those elements of spirit energy, kindness and compassion.

It can strike for the most innocuous of reasons. It is an emotion that sits there in a corner, watching you and saying, "One day you'll see me."

For this reason, I don't mind admitting that grief scares me, not least because on a daily basis I see it for real in the people that come to me for readings and in the people who come to my shows. But that doesn't mean that I become complacent about it, because I know how unbearable it would be if anything happened to one of my loved ones. Being a parent or grandparent, or a wife or husband, gives you a special window on what's at stake when you lose one of your family.

There are so many examples. One reading that I conducted that will always stay with me was for a lovely old lady who had lost her husband. They had never had children and lived in a cottage in the countryside. Their passion was gardening, and they grew all their own vegetables. Their lives reminded me of the rural idyll of that couple in the film *When the Wind Blows*, before the atomic bomb goes off.

I picked up the husband's energy and in my mind's eye I saw him sitting in the sun in his garden, surrounded by hollyhocks, buddleias and roses, with bees and butterflies dancing around him. I could feel the love he had for his wife and as I described the scene, I could feel her pain and longing. I always try to be professional in readings and have to distance myself from the emotion because it is not meant for me, but in this instance, I was in pieces. They had been married for over 60 years and had only known each other. They were almost the same person. Their energies were too tightly entwined to be pulled apart, even by death, and the lady explained that she had difficulty going out to tend their plants and vegetables, because she felt him there and it was too painful for her. She just wanted to die, because she had no reason to live anymore. Even the house, which had been their haven and sanctuary, had now become a prison where every room reminded her of what she'd lost. She could smell him on every towel and bedsheet.

They were such a traditional couple that he'd always taken care of the finances, and she was struggling because she'd never paid a bill in her life. From his energy I could see that he was desperately worried about her.

I knew nothing I could say would ever stop the pain she was feeling. All I could offer her was the comfort of knowing that her husband was with her in spirit and that she *should* go to the garden, because that's where their energies connected strongest and that's where she would feel him the most.

For me, as a medium, it never gets any easier when I see a client who is grieving; indeed as I've got older it affects me more, because the more I experience life the more I can relate. I honestly don't know how some people survive.

Sometimes, when I'm on stage, I pick up the energies of so many grieving people, I can't keep up, and one of the regrets I always have is that I can't give messages to everyone. What I do hope is that by seeing the messages and the validations that always happen when I perform, those in the audience who don't get a message can leave with the comfort of knowing that there is life after death and that they will see their loved ones again.

Although the exposure to grief that I experience through my work is hard, I view it as a huge privilege to be able to help those affected by loss. Death is such a personal, private thing. For all involved it is a life-changing moment, and to be allowed to be part of that, and to help those who are experiencing it, is humbling. It is why I always make sure that the messages I receive are honest and why no matter what those messages contain and how sensitive I might think they are, I can never self-edit.

In one reading I conducted for a bereaved wife, her husband in spirit gave the most random of messages.

"He said you emptied the tea in the sugar," I frowned.

The image I was receiving was of loose-leaf tea being emptied into a caddy of sugar.

"You were crying and you emptied the tea in the sugar," I expanded. "He was there. He saw you do it and he is worried about you."

This was one of those random pieces of information that means nothing to anyone apart from the person it is meant for. When she heard me say it, the woman broke down and sobbed. She admitted that she'd made the mix-up the previous day when she was unpacking the shopping and thinking about her husband. She hadn't told anyone. No one could have known. Such a weird piece of information gave her huge comfort though, because it confirmed to her that her husband's spirit was still there and watching over her.

On the other side of the life and death continuum, spirits also feel a kind of grief, because they feel the sadness and pain of their loved ones here on the Earth plane. They yearn to be able to comfort them, and to let them know they are at peace. That's why grieving people see so many signs. They are being love-bombed from the afterlife! But spirit grief is nothing like the grief we experience on Earth. Because spirits are in a place with such love, peace and serenity, they're happy.

If I can give those in spirit and those grieving for them a message that allows them to have the faith that what I am receiving is real and genuine, I can give peace of mind. The grief doesn't go, but the energy I connect with can help calm the rawness.

Another example where my connection to spirit energy has helped a grieving family will always stay with me.

It was the night I met Ellie and her family. She was a little girl who came through when I was performing in Norwich. There were over 1,000 people in the audience and by the time the reading finished, there was not a dry eye in the house.

I felt her as soon as I walked on stage and I knew straight away she was a young girl. I could sense she was around 10 or 11 years old, pretty, with mousy brown hair and sad brown eyes. My heart raced like it always does when there are children involved. I took a breath and spoke to the audience.

"I have a young girl here," I began, as I paced the stage. In my mind I could see and feel her and I opened up my mind to let her in. I could feel her energy being pulled towards a part of the audience. She wanted her mum. My heart ached.

"She wants her mum," I explained. "The name is Michelle."

Up in the circle a lady stood. She looked in her thirties and was attractive with blonde hair. Her eyes were filled with sadness. She was shaking.

Ellie was showing me images of her life. She was an active and fun-loving child.

"If I could, I would be running up and down this stage, darling," I told her.

It usually only takes that one hint of recognition for the floodgates to open and when Michelle heard my description she began to cry.

"My Ellie," she said.

Ellie's energy felt Mum's maternal tug and the connection was made. I felt a flood of warmth wash through me towards Michelle.

"Mummy, mummy," I repeated as the words dropped into my head. "I only went round the corner."

Hearing these words Michelle began to sob uncontrollably.

I didn't know it at the time, but Ellie was Michelle's daughter, Eloise. She had died just 15 weeks before the show and had been an animal lover and a horse rider. On the day of her death, she had been excited about taking her pony to a show and had gone out to feed and groom it in the fields behind her grandparents' house, where the pony was kept. As Ellie ran excitedly to her horse her mother was a few seconds behind her, just around the corner. But in a tragic accident, just before Michelle arrived, Ellie was kicked in the head by another horse which was excited by the food in her hand. The injury killed her.

"Where's my daddy, Andy?" I relayed. Ellie's energy was so strong I was picking up her mannerisms. I was talking like a young girl.

The man with Michelle, her husband and Ellie's father, stood up.

"That's me," he said. He was rubbing his wife's back, supporting and comforting her as he had done in the terrible weeks since their daughter's sudden death.

In my mind, Ellie took me to her house and showed me her bedroom, with the posters on the walls and photos of her on her horse. I saw her at the top of the stairs and she was singing, her beautiful voice belting out a pop song.

"You don't hear me singing, I sing at the top of the stairs. I call you."

Michelle nodded.

"Who's Peter?" I asked.

The man with Michelle and Andy stood. He was a family friend.

An image of a cut head snapped into my mind.

"Peter, head bleeding," I said. "Head bleeding."

Another woman with the group stood and explained that Peter's daughter had hurt her head.

"In my leg," I relayed to them. "Mummy they put something in my leg."

The spirit of the little girl was showing me scenes from after her accident. There were medical people around her and they were putting some kind of line into her leg. I could feel her panicking. She hated needles. "They said it would go away," Ellie's words flowed through my mind, "but it didn't go away."

Weeping, Michelle nodded. After the accident, as medics tried to save her life, they put injections in Ellie's leg; she didn't like needles and Michelle had always been haunted by the thought of that needle phobia and how Ellie would have been scared as they tried to save her life. She had told her daughter, "It's okay, they'll be gone soon."

By this point, I too was blinking back tears along with the family and most of the audience. I saw a cart in a field.

"In cart is where I sit," I explained to Michelle. "She is saying cart, not car."

"Yes, that's the horse cart," confirmed Michelle.

Ellie was telling her mum that was where she would be able to find the spirit of her daughter. "If you go out there you can feel me," she told her mum.

"I know where she means," nodded Michelle.

Then I saw locks of soft hair. Shiny and clean, I could smell fresh shampoo on it. It was child's hair. It was Ellie's hair, mousy brown and so silky I could almost feel it running through my fingers. I clenched my fists as if to hold it. I didn't want it to slip away, I wanted to feel this beautiful girl as if she were alive again, running through the fields with her hair blowing on the breeze, with a whole future ahead of her.

Then, pop! An image of hair in a freezer bag snapped into my mind.

"Her hair," I said. "Is it in a freezer bag?" I saw an image of Michelle silently closing a bag, her eyes heavy with sadness. I mimed closing a freezer bag. "Pop, pop, pop."

Michelle nodded again.

"I put it in a bag and then in a box," she wept. "I'm so frightened of losing her."

Then Ellie showed me another scene: her mum was at home tidying up and putting shiny buttons in a box; in the corner of the room stood Ellie, watching, full of love and longing. I knew this was a scene from after her death. Spirits are always drawn to the places they associate with love and this is especially so for children. Ellie had returned to her home and was watching her mum, hoping with all her energy that her mum could feel her presence.

"She was watching you," I told Michelle. "She'll show you signs. You'll hear her."

"I need to hear her," she replied.

Then, in the playful way child spirit often has, little Ellie showed me a comical scene of Peter, the family friend in the audience with her parents, desperately trying to pull on a pair of shoes that were too small for him. Ellie wanted to make her parents laugh, to ease their grief. She could see how emotional her mum was, and in that endearing way children have, she decided that the best way to make her feel better was to make her laugh.

I told Michelle what I was seeing in my mind and the group laughed and confirmed that Peter had indeed tried to wear a pair of shoes that did not fit.

As the audience laughed at the image, I felt Ellie's laughter tinkling in my ears.

"She thinks that is hysterical," I said. "Get a bigger pair of shoes Peter!"

As if her mum and dad still needed more validation, little Ellie gave them one more message. I saw a photo, a small passport-sized picture of Ellie grasped in her father's hand. I knew he often kissed it. It held so much energy, it held his love.

"Daddy has a photo," I said, repeating Ellie's words. "He kisses my photo." By this time, I was crying freely.

Andy let go of his wife and raised the palm of his hand for the theatre to see. Clutched inside was a small photo. Ellie, the girl whose spirit had amazed everyone, looked out from that picture.

It was one of the most powerful readings I've ever had the good fortune to deliver and everyone in the audience that night knew Ellie was there.

Of all the death that I deal with, I find it hardest to explain why children die. Why would anything divine just take away such innocence? It's a question I struggle with and to which I've still to find an answer. I have theories. Perhaps they have to go back to be reborn again. Perhaps they are the ones that become angels because their energy is still so pure. Whatever theories there are can never help explain to a parent why their child has died. No explanation can comfort a grieving parent, because they are left totally bereft and unable to cope with the agony of loss. In these situations, as in the reading for Ellie's parents, all I can do is pass on what I know, which is that when we die our physical presence isn't here anymore, but our spiritual presence in the form of our energy is. There are times during grief when nothing else is appropriate except this.

Sadly, for some, they will never get over their loss. The best they can do is learn to live with it.

Reactions to grief

Many years ago, a relative of mine lost his gran. She brought him up and they were more like mother and son. He was only in his early twenties when she passed, and he was devastated.

But thanks to what they call toxic masculinity nowadays, he bottled up his emotions until they needed an outlet somewhere. He couldn't cry because that wasn't what men did in those days. Instead, he was walking down a London street and had what I can only describe as a breakdown. While passing a bus garage late at night, he noticed a bus unattended but with the keys in the ignition and the engine running. He climbed in and went for a joyride. He drove it around like a lunatic and ended up crashing through the front of a shop in Kensington. He'd never been in trouble with the police before, had no criminal tendencies and up to that point had been a model citizen. In fact, after that, he became a fireman.

The police who arrested him were incredible, because they understood. They asked why and he said, "I dunno, I just lost it when Nan died."

That was enough of a reason for the magistrate to show leniency, too, when he was charged with the theft of a vehicle and criminal damage.

Learning about loss

Different people have very different reactions to grief. Some will even laugh when they are faced with sad news, not because they find it funny, but because of a psychological quirk. Studies say that this is a way for our subconscious to overcome fear and convince us that everything is actually okay. Sometimes we laugh because we're having trouble accepting what we see and are in shock, so we distance ourselves from the fear or pain by laughing it off.

The first time a lot of us experience grief is with the death of a family pet. This was how I first became acquainted with loss, when our dog died when I was a little girl. And I cried and cried. Back then, you were not really supposed to show grief, and from an early age children were conditioned to keep emotions in check, and face sadness with a stiff upper lip. I was told not to overreact and to just get on with it. My parents weren't being cruel, that's just how things were. But buried grief can't stay buried for long and if you're not allowed to express this rawest of emotions, it will find a way to come out somehow, or sit inside and fester and become a form of mental illness. Grief is the natural response to loss and should be expressed.

The next time I felt grief was when my nan died. I was bereft and was not in control of my emotions. It just came pouring out, all the tears, all the sadness.

As an appendix to this story, a few years later it transpired that she wasn't actually my birth nan, because her son wasn't my real father. When I realised this, the way I felt about her changed somewhat and although I still grieved her passing, missed her and loved her, it was as if she was placed in a different part of my heart and the grief was different.

Later in life, when my granddad died, who I adored, the grief was different again. At the time I had young children which gave me a focus and my life was changing. I was becoming a medium and I had started to understand much more about the afterlife, and I knew that although he was gone from the Earth plane, his energy was still around in another form. I felt his presence and still do, in the same way that many grieving people still feel the connection to their loved ones and call them their guardian angels.

Grief is hard, but you come through it. You feel like you can't survive but you do live with it. Eventually you remember the person and not the loss. You start to remember all the good stuff. Now, I can think of my granddad and I can laugh, but for years after his passing, when I thought about him I would cry.

Some people are lucky and hardly have grief in their life, and then you get others who just seem to have loss after loss. There is no rhyme or reason for this. If you have a lot of deaths in your life you will sadly experience a lot of grief. The only comfort I can give is that all those people have gone to a better place and they are still with you in spirit and in your heart. With time and, sadly, with frequency, you come to realise that you can survive grief and that realisation provides you with strength.

It's a bit like having children. The first birth is usually a huge shock: traumatic, scary and painful. You think it's never going to end, and that you can't cope. Subsequent births may not be any less painful or traumatic, but you are better prepared because you know what to expect and you also know that at some point, the pain will be over.

I think it's the same with grief. When I speak to people who have lost several loved ones, they will explain that while grief is always there, the knowledge that over time the pain changes and subsides gives them the comfort and strength to endure.

Grief and spirituality

Spirituality undoubtedly gives you the strength and fortitude to endure grief. The ability to access your spiritual capital and to tap into your faith and positivity allows you to recognise the possibility that a soul lives on and goes to a place where it resides and rests, surrounded by peace and love.

Once it's unlocked, spirituality is a form of inner strength that becomes an incredible balm against the pain of grief. Throughout history, people have turned to their spirituality to help them overcome pain, grief and hardship. Sometimes this takes the form of religious faith, other times it is a more esoteric spiritual strength. Spirituality helps grief heal and grief is a wound. Some days it is more painful than others and needs more attention and care. Some days you even forget it's there. Eventually, it becomes scar tissue. It is always there and is a part of you.

There are ways of making grief more bearable. One of the most important things to do is to continue to talk about the person that you're grieving for. Remembrance may be painful, but by talking about them and remembering them, we keep their energy connected to ours and we keep them in our hearts.

Some people find it unbearable to even discuss their lost loved ones and there are times in grief when all a person can do is shut out the pain. But talking does help.

People tend to be frightened of grieving people because death is a taboo. I have always found that grieving people will have at least one person in their life that runs away from them after they've lost a loved one, be that a partner, parent or child. I cannot tell you the amount of people who I encounter that explain that after they lost their husband, their best friend became distant. I've heard of people no longer being invited to barbecues or parties because their friends are worried that they will find it too hard being with a group of couples.

Grief frightens a lot of people, and they don't know how to handle it in others and what to do for the best. But we shouldn't fear people who are grieving, that's the worst thing you can do. Use the empathy you've developed through your spiritual practice to relate to that person.

If you've got a friend who's lost their loved one, you should talk to them, include them and always talk about your memories of them and their loved one together. Show them kindness and compassion. When you ignore people who are grieving, or try to gloss over their loss because you are worried you will upset them, this compounds their grief and makes them feel even lonelier.

Sometimes, it's human nature to change the subject, but don't. Go over and talk to them. Ask what happened, talk about their husband or wife; it will help, they will feel your empathy.

If you are the one who is grieving and you feel you cannot turn to friends or family, which can happen, I advise you to find somebody that is in the same place as you are, because it helps so much to have someone who has empathy and understanding of your situation. You need people who can relate to and support you. This is important because grief isolates people. If you are grieving, you need to share your voice and there are formal organisations who can help, such as Cruse Bereavement Care, ataloss.org, Widowed & Young and the Samaritans. Seeing a grief counsellor can also help. Don't lock your loss away.

The one thing that always frustrates me about death is that while we spend loads of energy preparing for new life, what with baby showers and NCT classes and endless trips to the shops to buy loads of baby stuff (most of which you don't need or ever use), we spend very little time preparing for death, even though it's inevitable. Indeed, we spend most of our time avoiding all talk or thought of it. And so, when it comes, which inevitably it does, we are unprepared both for the loss and the subsequent grief. Consequently, for most of us, death is more traumatic that it should be.

For this reason, I advocate having a grief first-aid kit for others that we can bring out and use when our friends or family suffer a bereavement. What I'm talking about here is a set of practices and behaviours that we can employ to help those we know when the inevitable does happen. It's more of a strategy than a box of plasters and bandages, although metaphorically that's exactly what it is, because it helps us dress the psychological wounds inflicted by grief.

The first thing to do is employ your innate kindness and show empathy. Check in on the person and make sure they have everything they need. When people suffer loss, all their energies are focused on their grief and often they struggle with the practicalities of life, like shopping, cooking and cleaning. This is where friends and family can help. Cook some meals for that person that can easily be heated up. Tidy up for them. When you go shopping, pick up a few bits and pieces.

If you've got a neighbour and they've lost their husband or wife, check in on them, take them some food, even if it's just a sandwich, because the last thing they're going to be thinking of is doing the shopping. Self-care goes out the window when grief comes through the door.

Vigilance is an important part of a grief first-aid kit. Keep an eye on those who have suffered loss. Are they losing weight, are they struggling? If you notice they need help, offer it. If you feel it's not your place, or if they shut themselves off, as some people do, try to get contact details from a friend or relative who they listen to.

Visit as much as you think is necessary, even if they don't let you in or do not want to talk. If this is the case drop them a note to let them know you are there if they need you. Just the knowledge that there are people who care can help grieving people.

If you meet someone in a social situation who has suffered a loss, talk about it, do not try to avoid the subject. If you knew the person who passed, share your memories. Keep the memory alive. Grief puts people in a bubble and often we feel so awkward and helpless that we try to avoid the subject completely. While you should not attempt to push any religious beliefs on a grieving person, on a spiritual level it is enough to know that memories keep energies connected, and so sharing memories and allowing the bereaved to reminisce about happy times helps them to keep the energy of their loved ones close.

Grief and Covid

Deaths from Covid create a certain type of grief reaction for a number of reasons. They often occur suddenly, so the families suffer a more acute sense of shock than those who have had time to prepare for a bereavement. In the early months of the pandemic many families were unable to be with their dying relatives, which led to frustration, anger and helplessness. Some people had to say goodbye to their loved ones over the phone, or via FaceTime. I can't fathom how much that hurts, not being able to touch or hold a loved one. Not being able to kiss them goodbye or be with them as they set off on their final journey.

And then, from a wider perspective, there are questions about government policies controlling hospitals and care homes. Could those deaths have been avoided? These concerns add to frustrations and can cause anger, resentment and a sense of injustice.

Much of the grief I've encountered through people who have come to me having lost loved ones through Covid is akin to those who have lost people in sudden accidents. There is shock and disbelief. One minute they are speaking to their loved one who has been taken into hospital suffering from the virus, the next minute they receive a call at 4am to say the person has passed.

"I was only talking to them a couple of hours before, Sally." I've heard that refrain so many times.

People often tell me that the events seemed to unfold in slow motion. That once that call is made to deliver the terrible news, everything seems to slow down, and nothing quite makes sense. That is the effect of disbelief. The brain can't comprehend what is happening, so perspective appears to slow down as you try to grasp the enormity of what's happening.

Grief causes shock even when you lose a loved one to a long-term or life-limiting illness, or someone who is elderly and frail. But an unexpected death caused by an unknown illness – as Covid was in the early days of the pandemic – creates a unique set of circumstances. For this reason, those who lost people to Covid in the first months of the pandemic and were unable even to have proper funerals because of lockdown, felt particularly alone. They were isolated physically and mentally, as they felt very few people could understand their circumstances.

I've heard of many people who developed a deep sense of anger and injustice against the government. Some seek revenge. One family I encountered through my work was adamant that they were going to hold someone to account and wanted to sue the NHS for what they believed were policy failings. They were angry at the system and looking for someone to blame. Their dad had Covid and was in hospital for many weeks; he was getting better but then took a turn for the worse and died suddenly. They tried to see him but couldn't.

Of course, it wasn't the hospital's fault, or the NHS. The staff and keyworkers were heroic, but sudden loss and grief makes people look for answers and someone to blame. Eventually, the family will begin to come to terms with what's happened, their anger will subside and they will become more realistic. Then they may be able to accept their loss. What they're really angry with is Covid. But you can't punish a virus and you can't get answers from a virus.

In their case, their sense of injustice towards the NHS may have been misguided, but often grief can give way to a sense of purpose, as in the cases of families who campaign for justice after the deaths of loved ones, such as Stephen Lawrence's parents, or the family of Jimmy Mizen who was murdered in an unprovoked attack in 2008. They established the Mizen Foundation, which campaigns against youth violence.

I am friends with Mitch Winehouse, Amy's father, and after her tragic death the family channelled their energies into setting up the Amy Winehouse Foundation, which today helps thousands of young people to better manage their emotional well-being.

Sudden death, and the death of young people, is disorientating and unfair, but the sense of frustration and injustice can often lead to renewed commitment and can provide kindness for others in the same situation, by offering a way to move forward with positivity, which are all keys to spirit power. Once again, spirit energy and our spiritual capital can give us the strength and faith to move beyond grief and turn loss into something positive.

Suicide

Grief comes in many guises which all cause a range of feelings, including pain, sorrow, loneliness and helplessness. People bereaved by suicide can have a particularly complicated set of feelings which create an even heavier burden on them.

There are several reasons for this. Suicide often leaves unanswered questions; it can lead to a sense of resentment towards the person who died, because survivors can feel abandoned, particularly partners and parents left to raise children on their own. In some cases, there is a religious element too, as several faiths including Catholicism and Islam view suicide as a sin.

Sadly, I frequently encounter both the families and the spirits of those affected by suicide, and in the vast majority of cases, the survivors are left with unanswered questions and are also full of guilt, which is a tragedy.

Suicide disproportionately affects men and is one of the biggest killers of men under 30. It takes real human kindness and empathy to be able to help those affected by suicide.

The first thing I can categorically say is that the spirits of those who have taken their own lives are at peace. Whatever was troubling them in life doesn't trouble them anymore.

The afterlife is the same for us all and the way we die does little to alter that. So, while some religions will say that people who take their own lives burn in hell, this isn't true. The only hell is the one faced by loved ones left here as they try to work out why that person took such a drastic final action and whether there was anything they could have done to stop them.

Suicide should be viewed as just another form of death, and while most people cannot fathom a situation where the best option appears to be taking your own life (unless the person in question is suffering intolerable pain), we must remember that those who take their lives were overpowered by depression and feelings of helplessness. There's no doubt that many people who end their own lives are suffering from mental illness, so while certain religions will tell us that it's wrong, if that person had instead died of cancer, they would not be so judging. Mental illness is the same as physical illness.

Suicide leaves families and loved ones looking for answers because it seems so surreal and unexplainable.

The spirits of those who have passed inevitably want to reassure those they left behind.

For example, I remember the spirit of a man who took his life and who appeared at a show a few years ago. His daughter was in the audience.

I saw a tragic scene that had played out several days before his death when he had tried to kill himself but did not succeed. He tried to hang himself at the bottom of a staircase and I explained this to his daughter, who nodded and confirmed that they lived in a pub and that her dad had tried to commit suicide in the cellar.

"He couldn't cope, he was under so much pressure," she explained.

The man wanted his daughter to know that he was at peace.

Suicide leaves so many questions, even when the person leaves a note. This is because suicide is a secretive moment. It is a lonely pact between that person and their thoughts. It will never be totally understandable to those who are left behind.

More recently, I did a reading for a woman with had two young children, one of whom had found the body of his father in the garage after he had killed himself. The woman was confused and angry.

"We were just having a normal day," she explained. "We were planning a barbecue and my husband went into the garage to get something. When he had been a while, my son went to find him. He'll never get over finding his daddy like that."

Her husband had planned it. Suicide is rarely a spur of the moment decision. He put everything he needed away in the garage and waited for the opportunity.

His wife told me that he had struggled all his life with mental health problems and had always had very low self-esteem. He believed he had no worth and that he was always letting people down. She admitted that the strain had nearly split up the family many times.

"No matter what I said to him to try and make him believe in himself he would always look for things to justify how bad he was feeling," she explained.

And while she tried to understand the illness that made him do what he did, she couldn't help feeling angry at him for the position he'd put their son in. It was a desperately sad situation. On the one hand she missed her husband and grieved for him, and on the other she was angry at him and was struggling to forgive him.

Suicide affects everyone it touches. It can have a ripple effect, extending well beyond the person's immediate family and friends. There are many examples of people being affected by the suicides of people they never knew, and in very extreme cases there can be copycat deaths, as happened in the county of Bridgend in Wales several years ago, when scores of young people started to take their own lives, leaving parents terrified and experts mystified.

The Welsh Assembly claimed the 'spate' only took place in 2007 and 2008. The official number of suicides was 23. However, the deaths continued far beyond that timeframe and reports suggested that in the five years up to February 2012, 79 people took their lives in and around Bridgend. There were rumours of internet suicide cults and pacts and even a conspiracy theory that suggested young minds had been damaged by radio frequencies. All the outlandish explanations were fantasy.

As the death toll increased, an anti-suicide task force made up of health and education officials was launched. Groups from local youth clubs were taken away for weekends where they were counselled. The mainstream media were asked to stop reporting on the phenomenon to try to stop copycat behaviour. But social media helped spread the word and the dead were given emotional online memorials. Gradually, as the years went on, the numbers normalised.

Sociologists agree that what happened was a rare suicide cluster and that the deaths spread by behavioural contagion. Throughout history there have been similar events. In the month following Marilyn Monroe's overdose, 197 suicides were recorded, mostly of young blonde women who appeared to have used the movie icon's death as a model for their own. The theory that suicidal behaviour can spread is known as the Werther Effect, named after the tragic character in the classic book *The Sorrows of Young Werther* by Goethe. In the story, Werther takes his life in a specific way and after the book was published in 1774, people started imitating his actions.

In September 2015, Public Health England issued a report to agencies about suicide clusters and how to deal with them. The report explained the role that social media can play in developing clusters, stating that suicidal behaviour is increasingly spreading via the internet. It warned that social media can cause a greater number of suicides to occur in a specific time period and to spread out geographically in 'mass clusters'. For this reason it's important, particularly for the young, to be aware of the unforeseen effects of suicide.

Dealing with grief

Initially, when grief is raw, people experience pain, shock, bewilderment, confusion and sometimes denial. Often the hardest thing to accept is that the person is gone. Faith in spirit and in the afterlife can help, but it still doesn't stop the pain. Some people report a period of complete calm, almost euphoria, which I think is your spirit energy flooding your body to protect you from these overpowering feelings.

People learn to live with loss, and they learn to cope without the person they are grieving for, but there are always reminders. There will be certain places, smells, sights, sounds, songs and even people that trigger memories. These often come totally out of the blue, and the emotional freefall begins over again. It presents itself in many ways: crying, not eating, becoming withdrawn. Sometimes good, happy memories are sent as signs from those in spirit.

Later, the process of moving on begins. It starts with practical actions such as removing your loved one's name from your bills or your joint accounts. This stage is fraught with guilt. You feel like you are letting that person down, deserting them in some way. Do not worry. They understand.

If there are items that you feel you need to remove, such as photographs that are too painful to look at, store them in a memory box until you feel stronger and more able to concentrate on the good, happy memories. No one should ever be forced to get rid of personal belongings and things that were precious to the person who has died. These can hold residues of their spirit energy and provide an important link to their spirit. Bereaved people need to be able to take their time. I feel sad when I hear about people who have bagged up someone's belongings soon after they died and taken them all to the charity shop or auctioned them off on eBay. I guarantee that in those circumstances, a few weeks or months down the road there will be regret. If you feel the need to remove belongings, perhaps ask another member of the family if they would like them instead of throwing them out completely.

That said, it is not always good for bereaved people to surround themselves with mementos, as they can sometimes stop us from moving forward.

There are lots of other ways to keep memories. When we have children, we should pass down anecdotes and stories that were passed down to us about our family. My grandfather used to tell me about his adventures as a stall holder selling strawberries outside Southfields station in south-west London. He would recount all the banter and the scrapes he got into. I would crack up. I told the same stories to my children when they were little, and they now tell them to their children. It keeps Granddad George alive.

Indeed, storytelling is universal and is as old as humankind. Before there was writing there was storytelling; it occurs in every culture, to entertain, inform and pass down traditions, stories and values through the generations: a collective memory of past events passed down through time. The Choctaw Native American tribe, for example, have a storytelling tradition going back generations. Their stories were intended to preserve the tribe's history and educate the young.

The way we remember our loved ones is incredibly personal. What we decide to keep is an individual choice. I have a friend whose husband died young. He was in his thirties and he fell off some scaffolding. Years later, she met a new man and moved in with him. They were very happy. But she had all her former husband's clothes in boxes in the garage and one day she asked me for some advice. Should she get rid of them? I explained that it shouldn't bother her new partner. She said that every now and then she felt her husband around her and walking in the garage kept him alive in her head. So she kept it all.

For people who lose a spouse or a partner, the final piece of letting go can be when they decide to have another relationship. Again, this decision will be full of questions and doubts and again the decision is up to the individual. There are no hard and fast rules.

Practicalities of loss

I'm finishing this chapter with some advice which, while not necessarily spiritual, can help with grief and so allow people the space to heal.

I wanted to include this because following the pandemic, and the sudden death toll it caused, I've encountered many people who were unprepared for the death of a loved one and who had to deal with lots of financial and legal problems at a time when they were least able to think logically.

For this reason, I always advise people to make a will and to ensure that in the event of their sudden death, there is a record of their final wishes. I'd even go so far as to advise people to make sure that if they want their loved ones to be financially secure, they should get the relevant life insurance policies in place.

There is a huge practical and bureaucratic side to death that people struggle with and are generally unprepared for. A will is so important, or even simply some sort of letter that sets out your wishes, but it's something that we overlook because we are too scared to think about our own mortality. And the lack of guidance for those left behind can cause so many problems.

I saw one client whose father had died in the pandemic. He was elderly and she had been caring for him, but he hadn't left a proper will, even though he'd expressed a wish on many occasions that he wanted his daughter, rather than his son, to inherit his house and to split the rest of his estate down the middle. He'd explained this to both of them.

After he died it transpired that there was no legally binding document to enact his wishes and even though there was agreement, the son decided he wanted half of the house. The siblings fell out over the issue at a time when they should have been grieving together.

It is such a common issue. In another case there were four siblings, one of whom had been cut out of his mother's will, while his sisters had been told by their mum that the estate would be split into thirds for them in the event of the old lady's demise. The siblings all knew that their mother was a vindictive and manipulative woman who, after the death of her husband, used the will and the threat of exclusion as a way of controlling her children. Anyone who disagreed with her or stood up to her and didn't do what she wanted would be cut out of the will. Her only son fell foul of her temper when he stood up to her one day. She told him she never wanted to see him again and wrote him out of the will. She told her daughters what she'd done, hoping the action would keep them in line. But the four adult siblings all talked and understood what she was like, so they agreed that in the event of their mother's death, they would split everything four ways. The agreement was made and stood for many years but was never formalised in any contract or legal document.

You can guess what's coming next.

The old lady died and by the time she'd passed, her daughters had all but abandoned her. They all lived away and rarely saw her. She died a sad, lonely old lady, having pushed all her family away. In the last years of her life, she relied on carers, and even when her grandchildren tried to intervene and help, she became paranoid that they were only helping to try to get hold of her precious riches. She died alone one Boxing Day, having spent Christmas Day on her own. As she had promised, her estate was left to her three daughters. There was nothing for her son, who by that stage had not seen or spoken to her for 10 years.

After the funeral, which was done as cheaply as the family could manage, the will was read and the son expected his sisters to make good on their promise. They had other plans however. One of them was widowed and her husband had died penniless, leaving her with nothing. One had emigrated and didn't even attend the funeral, while the third was a spinster who was still renting and had never been able to afford her own home. Together they argued that their brother, who had a home and a decent pension, didn't need the money. So they cut him out and reneged on their agreement.

The epilogue to this rather tragic story is that the old lady, who left a considerable amount of money, had inadvertently been claiming lots of benefits she wasn't entitled to. Her son had set these up for her when his father was still alive, and because she shut him out of her life and the daughters had little to do with her, they continued being paid. When she died, the error was uncovered and after many months of investigation, the government took back all the money that had been overpaid from her estate, which ran into thousands of pounds.

So, my advice is make a will and put your wishes in writing. If you can afford it, put them in the form of a legal contact. It can literally keep a family together in times of loss.

Even if you think you've got nothing, because perhaps you rent and don't have any savings, you may still have possessions that your family might argue over when you die. In my experience, there's always going to be something that a relative might feel they are entitled to. Make your wishes clear because the people left behind will appreciate it.

Chapter 9

Energise yourself

Spirit and body are intrinsically linked. The healthier our bodies are, the more ability we have to nourish our spirit energy. If we are healthy mentally and physically – we can share and spread love.

The natural mindset of anyone who is spiritually strong is one of positivity, faith, kindness and purpose, all of which have been shown to have a beneficial impact on health.

Positive thinking is how you reflect on life. It is your outlook and your attitude toward yourself and your life. It's commonly summed up as glass half full or glass half empty, or optimistic or pessimistic.

As I've explained previously, positivity is one of your keys for unlocking your spirit energy and studies show that this personality trait affects many areas of health and well-being and helps to manage stress. When facing a health crisis, for example, actively cultivating positive emotions can boost the immune system and counter depression. Studies have shown an indisputable link between having a positive outlook and health benefits like lower blood pressure, less heart disease, better weight control and healthier blood sugar levels.

For example, one study by the University of California, San Francisco, found that people with new diagnoses of HIV infection who practised a set of skills designed to promote positivity carried a lower load of the virus, were more likely to take their medication correctly and were less likely to need antidepressants to help them cope with their illness. The researchers studied 159 people who had recently learned they had HIV and randomly assigned them to either a positive emotions training course or general support sessions. 15 months later, those trained in positivity skills maintained higher levels of positive feelings and fewer negative thoughts about their infection, improving both their physical and mental health.

It is important to understand that positive thinking doesn't mean that you ignore bad situations. These are unavoidable in life. Instead, positive thinking just means that you approach unpleasantness in a more positive and productive way by thinking the best is going to happen, not the worst, and by accepting that unpleasantness isn't a permanent state. Bad things pass, as do good things. The trick is to try to keep a balance, take every opportunity to enjoy the good as much as you can and be resilient to the bad stuff.

Faith has also been linked to better health. Studies have shown it to be associated with better health outcomes, including greater longevity, coping skills and health-related quality of life, even during terminal illness. Having faith in a higher power reduces anxiety, depression and suicide. It has also been shown that addressing the spiritual needs of a patient may enhance recovery from illness.

Meanwhile, kindness is also a health-boosting property, with one study showing that multiple sclerosis sufferers who helped others benefitted more than those who only received help. Kindness has been shown to increase self-esteem, empathy and compassion – and improve mood. It can decrease blood pressure and inhibit the production of cortisol, a stress hormone, which directly impacts stress levels.

Purpose is a gateway to better health. One study by researchers at the University of California, San Diego, suggested that if you feel you have a purpose in life, your physical and mental health improves. The study surveyed more than 1,000 adults and found that people who felt that they had meaning in their lives were more likely to feel physically and mentally healthy, while those who were 'searching' for meaning were less likely to feel that way. These associations were particularly strong among older people in the study.

Finally, from our spirit energy keys, grounding yourself in the present is also a surprisingly powerful way to boost your health. This particularly applies to mental health and is achieved most effectively through the practice of meditation, which in essence is a way to bring our mind to the present moment and filter out all the noise that distracts us and diverts our attention.

It's amazing just how much time and effort we put into not living in the here and now, which means for a lot of the time we're not even here, psychologically speaking! Our minds have so much to be distracted by and our collective attention has wandered even more since the advent of the ubiquitous smartphone. In one study, people said their minds wandered to think about something unrelated to their current experience for almost 50 per cent of the time. Which basically means that, half the time, most of us are not thinking about now – we're thinking about something else. The same study also found that people reported being less happy when their minds wandered.

I like to think of the mind as being like a badly behaved dog on a lead that constantly wanders off and needs to be pulled back to heel.

Scientific study has shown that meditation, which includes things such as yoga and chanting, is a powerful tool against a range of health problems. It's believed that the calm state reached through meditation makes the brain subconsciously alter the sympathetic nervous system – the part that responds to stress – and as a result lowers our heart rate, respiratory rate and blood pressure. One of the biggest studies of its kind, presented to the American Heart Association, found patients with coronary heart disease who practised meditation and chanting had nearly 50 per cent lower rates of heart attack, stroke and early death compared to non-meditating subjects. The nine-year research followed men and women with narrowing arteries in their hearts who were randomly assigned to either practise meditation or to participate in a control group which was given health education classes in traditional risk factors, including diet and exercise.

Another study found chanting helped lower blood pressure after three months of regular practice and surmised that students who were at risk of developing hypertension saw the possibility drop significantly if they continued chanting.

Other studies even suggest that mediation can change the shape and structure of the brain. Scientists have discovered that animals and humans that experience stressful events in early life have a larger amygdala, the part of the brain that processes fear and threat. One found that that the amygdala shrunk slightly during an eight-week meditation programme, while another found a link between meditation, reduced inflammation and improved responses to stress.

As you can see, there's a lot of science to back up my assertion that adopting a spiritual lifestyle based on the six keys we have covered can leave you healthier and help boost your overall well-being.

One yogic practice I wouldn't recommend, however, is the practice of khechari mudra, which teaches yoga monks to lengthen their tongues by stretching and slicing through the frenulum, the piece of skin under your tongue which anchors it to the bottom of your mouth. Do not try this at home!

With practice, a monk who masters this skill is able to roll his tongue to the back of his mouth and insert it into his nasal passage. Why would he want to do this?

Because it's believed that if you can touch the very back of your nasal cavity with your tongue you can stimulate your pituitary gland, which then releases a liquid thought to be a kind of spiritual nectar. It's really just a mix of mucus and saliva. Khechari mudra, mixed with bhramari pranayama – a form of humming meditation – is believed to help with hearing loss and dementia.

But it's not just these well-researched links between the elements of spirit power and health that prove living a more spiritual life is good for you. The energy of spirits that have passed over will also always do its best to ensure the well-being of their loved ones left here, which is why we should always be vigilant for the signs they send us.

Most people that speak to me about the loss of a loved one will be concerned about the welfare of the one who has passed.

"Are they okay?" is the first question I am always asked. It works the other way round, too.

For example, very recently I did a reading for an Australian woman who had lost her husband.

It took place during the pandemic, and we made contact via video. She was in her forties and looked tired when we connected. She explained that it had been a very tough few weeks because an elderly member of her family was ill and she had been looking after him, travelling backwards and forwards between homes. She didn't mention her husband, or the circumstances of his death, but I sensed him straight away.

"I have a man here, he's young. He's in spirit and he died several years ago. He's very worried about you," I explained.

She knew straight away who I was talking about.

"I have the name Graham?" I offered.

She nodded.

"He was my husband," she confirmed.

I could hear Graham's words in my head. He spoke with a heavy Australian accent and he was telling his wife she needed to rest.

"He says you are doing too much, that you need to look after yourself and slow down," I relayed. "He says you can't save everyone."

The images in my mind then switched to a scene in a hospital. I saw Graham hooked up to machines that were keeping him alive. His wife, younger by many years, was there at his side, holding his hand and crying.

"He knew you were there," I told her. "He knew you were with him at the end and he took great comfort in that."

The woman was crying.

"He just wants to know that you are okay and most of all he wants you to be happy and healthy, because he wasn't, and he regrets not looking after himself."

I could see it all. Graham was a heavy drinker and a drug user when he was alive. He had an abusive childhood and this had sent him spiralling into a lifetime of mental health problems. His wife had also suffered mental illness and depression and at times they'd enabled each other's drug habits. Graham's had eventually killed him. He overdosed and fell into a coma, which eventually led to brain death. His wife was there when they switched off his life support.

She confirmed all I was picking up.

"It made me so sad, thinking that he didn't know I was there at the end because his brain was dead," she said.

"But his spirit was there, and it was connected to you. He could feel you as he passed," I explained. "He is at peace. He isn't suffering anymore. They don't carry the pain or the anguish. You have to let your guilt go now too and start living for yourself."

It was an incredibly emotional reading and I hope it proved cathartic for the lady and gave her closure, as I sensed her life had been in limbo for many years, with her health suffering as a result.

People often ask me if I get affected by the things I see and feel when I work. It is true, I see some dreadful things and often they are accompanied by physical feelings. For example in another recent reading I picked up the spirit of a woman who had been shot in the head during the war in the Balkans. I could actually feel what it was like having a bullet wound in the back of my head. It's hard to explain. I didn't experience the sort of pain or trauma that you would associate with a gunshot wound, but I certainly knew what it was. It was an experience – a feeling. It was there momentarily. It happens frequently. Spirits project their ailments and injuries on me in order to offer their loved ones validation, and although it can be unpleasant, it doesn't affect me. I've got used to this over the years.

In fact, our loved ones never mean us any harm and care deeply for us, even from spirit, where they can see what life has in store for us and can foretell any problems we may experience in the future. This is not because death suddenly allows spirits to see into the future, although premonitions are sometimes enabled by spirit energy. No, the reason our loved ones in spirit can predict impending health problems is because when they connect with us, they are attuned to our spirit energy. And through this they can sense if there are problems on the horizon.

I know this for a fact, because I was warned about an impending personal health disaster by a loved one in spirit several years ago.

It happened just as I was preparing to go on stage for a show. For several months I'd had a niggling ache in my hips and knees. This was before I had weight-loss surgery and at the time, I was morbidly obese. I wore size 26 to 28 clothes and although it never really bothered me psychologically, as I was happy and confident, it had started to take a physical toll on me.

At the time, I was on the road, spending up to four nights a week on stage on my feet and more hours than I care to remember cooped up in cars between venues. As a consequence, my hips had really started playing up. Most nights I'd reach the stage wings puffing. I'd have to stand there and catch my breath before going on stage.

On the night in question, as I stood in the darkness catching my breath and trying to shift around to ease the ache, I sensed a voice in spirit louder and clearer than the others that were waiting to connect with the audience. It reverberated around in my mind repeatedly.

"You can't go on like this Sally, you can't go on like this Sally," it said.

I remember it so clearly. It was a male voice, stern and authoritative, but also full of love and concern. And I knew straight away who it was. It was Granddad George, the spirit I like to think of as my guardian angel.

He was warning me that I'd reached the limit of what my body could cope with and that if I didn't do something drastic and quickly, I'd be joining him in spirit. It was like a light coming on in my head. It was my epiphany, and it was the moment I realised that my weight was killing me.

The very next day I called a clinic which specialised in weight-loss surgery and several months later I went under the knife to have a gastric bypass. If I hadn't had that surgery, I have no doubt that I would be dead now. I had already suffered one minor heart attack and I was on the way to another.

So, while our health issues are earthly matters, spirits can come to us and warn us about them, because they do not want to see us suffer.

Another example of this happened in the north of England at a show when a man called Jim, who was in spirit and connected to his niece who was in the audience, and very much alive, told her, "Do not cancel your X-ray!"

Jim also told a nephew who was there to be careful of his diet and to cut down on dairy.

Jim had quite obviously been keeping an eye on his family from spirit.

When we do become unwell, spirits come to us and care for us.

At another show, I remember a lady took a message from a woman in spirit called Wendy.

"She was my best friend," the lady in the audience explained.

As I was picking her energy up, I felt a strange trembling sensation down my right side and asked the lady what it meant.

She explained that she had just been diagnosed with Parkinson's Disease. Her friend was coming through for her to reassure her.

One of the most amazing recent stage readings I was involved in happened just before the Covid lockdown and illustrated just how quickly spirits can jump between life and death.

A family of sisters was sitting a couple of rows from the front. In the first half of the show they had been watching intently, but hadn't got any messages. In the second half I noticed a couple of them hadn't returned.

I was picking up an energy and could sense the name Paul. He was directing me towards the area of the theatre where the women were seated.

I walked to their side of the stage.

"I have a Paul here," I said. "He's recently passed." And then I paused. There was something unusual about his energy.

"Or maybe he's not quite in spirit yet," I said.

I felt that he was hovering somewhere, not quite alive or dead. Don't ask me how I knew, I just did.

There was a gasp from the group and one of the women put her hand up.

"He just died," she said.

"What?" I was confused.

"In the break," she explained.

For one awful moment I thought she meant someone had died in the theatre.

"Oh my God!" I shrieked. "Where?"

"He was in hospital," she said. "He's an old friend and was very ill. That's where the others went. They've gone to the hospital. We were expecting it any time. We got a text just before the show started again to say he'd passed away."

I couldn't believe it.

"Well, he's come straight here to tell you he's okay now," I told them. I asked them whether they needed to go too.

"No, we wanted to stay and see the rest of the show," they said.

Despite the sadness of their friend's passing, they could also see the funny side of the situation, as could the rest of the audience. Sometimes you have to laugh.

It illustrated just how quickly people can come through. In the past I've heard other so-called mediums explain to people that the reason they cannot connect with their recently departed is that it takes time for spirits to mature, as if there's a gestation period between life and death. I don't agree. I think it's up to the spirit and each one is different. We are all unique in life, so why not in death. Why would we suddenly change and all become the same? Every single energy and spirit is unique.

* * *

One final thing to mention while I'm discussing spiritual health, is how to comfort somebody who is terminally ill and nearing the end of life. Sadly, this is something that a lot of people face.

Firstly, there are general common-sense things to take into account, such as making them as comfortable as possible and allowing them to rest when they need to. There can be a temptation to try to feed people because we associate food with strength, but if a person is gravely ill and cannot eat, don't force food on them. Sometimes they just need peace and quiet and sleep. The most important thing is reassurance and company. This is where your kindness, compassion and faith come in. Let them know that they are going to be okay, and that they will see their loved ones again.

I have to say that a lot to people who are facing death, or who have relatives and friends with life-limiting illness, and I say it with confidence because I know it's true. Honesty can be hard. The natural reaction we have when faced with someone who is terminally ill is to try to cheer them up, or to divert their attention from the fate that awaits them. But often this isn't what they need. If they have accepted what is happening to them, they need the comfort and peace of mind that knowing that death isn't the end brings them.

Most importantly, treat them the same as you have always treated them. Don't avoid them, be there for them and let them know you are there for them.

10

Finding your happy place

Lots of guides will tell you that it's good to have goals, and many people set themselves targets and objectives. They have five-year plans and even 10-year plans. They look far into the future, visualise what they want, strategise how to get it and then set a deadline. Some will work out a firm plan of action and not deviate from it; others will hope that just the act of wanting a specific goal or thing is enough to magically make it materialise. The plan becomes a roadmap, a blueprint by which to live their life.

For many, this way of living works just fine. It's better than drifting along with no direction, they argue. They may be right; after all, purpose is one of the spirit energy keys.

But here's the glitch in this very common life-strategy. The goals that are set rarely include happiness as a primary element. They are professional goals, or personal goals that may or may not lead to some happiness as a bonus. A promotion, a relationship, weight loss, a bigger house or a new car.

I would argue that long-term happiness in itself should be the goal, and that anything else is a bonus, because if we are not happy, we are either in a neutral emotional state, or we are unhappy.

Instead, the general compulsion in life is to seek happiness in short-lived pleasures. We seek out pleasurable experiences for our senses, such as food, booze, box sets. We get a promotion at work and enjoy the sense of achievement for a week or so. The pursuit of happiness becomes a quest and we are always looking for the next thing, jumping from experience to experience, chasing pleasure and trying to avoid pain. Happiness becomes a repetition of pleasant, short experiences.

I'm just as guilty of this as everyone else. I'm a sucker for a new frock or a handbag and enjoy eating out.

But what if there's another way to be happy that doesn't involve chasing pleasure? What if we can be happy without having to create pleasure for ourselves by attaining life goals, or spending money on objects or dazzling our senses with experiences? What if happiness doesn't rely on gratification?

That, in essence, is what spirit energy can provide for you.

Living life according to the six keys of spirit energy sets you on the path of a happiness that is much deeper than the happiness most of us recognise. A life where the primary values are faith, kindness, positivity, purpose, authenticity and being in the present is a life with happiness embedded in it.

If you gain happiness from your values, you free yourself from the need to seek happiness externally. If your values and behaviour become the source of your happiness and well-being, you get off the treadmill and stop chasing external pleasure, because it's all within you.

That's one of the key lessons of spirituality. The key to a better life is inside all of us. That infinite energy source, which is made of love and giving and which can be accessed with the right keys, is available to everyone. You don't need money or your name on a guest list. Everyone is welcome!

If we are all honest, deep down we know this to be the truth. Although wealth and fame can give access to many forms of pleasure, few of us have any illusions that they guarantee long-term lasting happiness. The proof is there to read in every tabloid and celebrity magazine, because even if only a tiny percentage of what's written about reality stars, soap actors, politicians or sports people is true, their lives are far from perfect. Trust me, I've met many of them. Their lives are sometimes more miserable and chaotic than the lives of 'normal people', by which I mean non-famous people. Fame, fortune and success do not provide an inoculation against problems. Even so, you ask a lot of young people what they want in life and the simple answer is "to be famous". It is fool's gold.

True realistic happiness is an inner strength. It's not created by bling. It's been studied in the world of psychology, and even governments pay close attention to the happiness levels of populations, because happy people are healthier.

In the past decade in the UK there has been a happiness revolution. Workplaces recognise that happy people are more productive and schools understand that happy pupils learn better and go on to become more engaged and industrious citizens.

This drive to understand, improve and define happiness has also spawned a self-help movement. Evidence-based positive psychologists, scientists and academics warn that you shouldn't make happiness your goal and that the modern-day preoccupation with finding happiness at all costs, all of the time, will, in fact, lead to misery, because, largely, life isn't constantly happy.

Finding your happy place

In this school of thought the secret to happiness is not the search for happiness, but rather the ability to cope with unhappiness instead; happiness doesn't come from material things or pleasure, it comes from traits such as resilience, stoicism, self-reliance and confidence.

If you've never encountered stoicism before, it is certainly worth investigating. It's basically the posh name for the character trait we call a stiff upper lip. Stoicism is a school of philosophy that flourished in ancient Greece and Rome and is grounded in the idea that life is difficult. One of its main themes is the rejection of hope in the face of adversity, with the caveat that although things are likely to get bad, they will eventually improve.

One of the core elements of stoicism is that mental well-being is based on the judgements we make about things, rather than the things themselves, and that unhappiness and mental suffering result from swift value judgements. We can't change the world, we can't make everyone like us and we can't use the power of positive thinking to make things better. But at the same time, our well-being is dependent on how we think about things and how we assess the situations we are in.

What this really means is that happiness is within our grasp, but not through the things we find in the external world. The key is to view adversity as a test that we can learn from to build resilience for the future. So, while there is no point in sugar-coating problems and difficulties, we can at least comfort ourselves with the fact that we will emerge from them a bit bruised, but wiser and stronger.

Part of our spiritual happiness, then, is about learning to accept that life isn't always perfect. You will have bad times, you will be sad, you will suffer and you will experience loss. Even for extraordinarily lucky people, life gets difficult at times. Once you can accept this, however, the negativity associated with pain and difficult situations begins to lose its power. And when you add faith into the mix, you begin to understand that hardship is generally temporary, because life is not lived in one constant state. We ebb and flow through different states and different circumstances.

Life is about change.

Oddly, people fear change, but without it, we'd be stuck in the same place. We should be embracing change because once you understand that every situation is temporary, you start to realise that unhappiness ends, and that nothing bad lasts forever.

Life is a journey through the world. To a large degree we have free will to choose where we go and how we get there, but the one unavoidable and ultimate destination here on Earth for everyone is death. It gets us all in the end. Most people fear it and do their best to ignore it, but acceptance of death and the faith that there is something else beyond it will free you from fear and enhance your happiness – and happiness is vital for your spirituality because the divine power that gives us our spirit energy wants us to be happy.

That's why I sometimes have problems with religions that include elements of anger, guilt, misery, fear. None of those have a place in the spirituality I practise, and I struggle to understand why representations of gods in other religions would want to promote fear, or guilt or intolerance. Surely if there is a god up there, he'd want everyone to be happy? If there really is that bloke up there on a cloud with a beard, I would hope that he loves us and is more of a kind uncle than a tyrant holding a lightning bolt.

Now we've established that happy people have strong spirit energy, the next step is to discover what makes you happy personally. We are talking about spiritual happiness here, so it can't be a new car, or a pair of shoes.

For me personally, if I want to be happy I stop and take a deep breath and I think about everything I have gratitude for. I think about my family, and I think about all the ways I am lucky. I have my health. I have my purpose. I have my loved ones and my friends. And when someone or something is making me unhappy, I stop, I take a breath and I give that unhappiness back. I don't own anyone else's anger or hate. It's a trick we can all do. You give the negativity back with your mind, you refuse to take it on. It took me years to learn this trick, and I would worry about what people thought of me and what they were saying. I would take it on, and it then became a burden. Now I have a different mindset. What people think of me is their business, not mine. I'm happy in myself and I love myself, so I don't need validation from someone else.

I have reached a place of contentment. This brings peace of mind, which gives me happiness.

But happiness comes in many guises, and we would all do well to take it where we can find it. Just before I wrote this section of the book, I was dealing with one of the usual day-to-day service problems we all face. This one was with a bank. Inevitably, it involved a long wait to get through to someone in a call centre, who then had to elevate my query to someone else. It is just one of the tiresome factors of modern life. To get anything done within the service industry inevitably involves a headache nowadays. It could have sent me right over the edge and ruined my morning, if not my whole day.

But I persevered, I stuck to my guns but was polite and respectful, and in the end, I got a satisfactory result and had a laugh with the person on the other end of the line.

It took two hours. I had every right to be frustrated but chose instead to be happy because I resolved the problem. That's what I mean about taking happiness where you can find it. Quite often, problems can be reframed as wins if we face them with tools from our spirit-energy armoury and resolve them. And that provides a reason to be happy.

Happiness doesn't have to be about the big things in life. Small wins can make you just as happy as big ones, like when you find money in the pocket of a jacket that you haven't worn for a while. You feel like you've won the money, even though it always belonged to you.

Happiness and laughter make life worth living, so it makes sense to find the things that make you happy and make time for them. One of my pleasures in life is singing. People tell me they always know what mood I'm in because if they hear me singing, they know I'm happy. I'm no professional by any stretch but I don't really care. It just makes me happy. If I'm a bit down, I'll say to John, "I've not sung for a couple of days" and I'll knock out a tune. I have had moments in my life where I've been so down and thought, "I haven't sung for weeks." And then, all of a sudden, I find myself singing and I'm out of it. And that is the truth. I can sing the blues away.

Indeed, if you have to have goals, make one of them to laugh every day. A good sense of humour is one of the most important things you can develop in life because not only does it protect you against sadness and help you find happiness, it also makes you a more attractive person. There's a reason why so many profiles on dating sites include the letters GSOH (good sense of humour).

I've always been able to find the humour in things, even when I was a little girl and used to laugh at the name of Mr and Mrs Fish, who lived across the road.

We should always strive to be happy and allow spirituality to make us happy, but be realistic and aware that there will be times of unhappiness. This is the most realistic and healthy way to find happiness. And happiness does makes us healthy, because it defends us against mental health problems.

We should also see it as part of our spiritual duty to try to make those around us happy, too. This involves using intuition to discover the source of their unhappiness, and empathy to put yourself in their shoes and to understand why they are feeling the way they are. It might be very simple to identify the source of their unhappiness; they may be ill, or their relationship may have broken down.

Sometimes, however, the source of their unhappiness may lie deeper and, in these cases, you need to talk to them and let them know they can trust you. Often, you will not be able to directly cure the cause of the unhappiness, but being there for someone, understanding what they are going through and supporting them, is enough to help.

In the world today we have many more things that can make us both happy and unhappy. Social media is a great example. A lot has been written about the negative effects. The online bullying, the 'trolling', the misinformation it can spread. But it is also worth noting that social media can make you happy, too, because it allows people to connect to each other in ways that were not possible before. You've only got to consider what happened in those long months of lockdown to realise that there is potential to find happiness in social media. It was the only way many families could connect and, in a world where families are often divided by distance, the technology bridges the geographic gap.

It is popular to bash social media, but I look at it in a more objective way. Social media itself isn't the problem, it's the people who use it. If we all deployed our spirit energy keys when we logged on, the online space would largely be a happy space. Like so many things in life, when something can make you miserable, it also has the potential to make you happy. Social media can really bring out the worst in people and therefore make others unhappy. But at the same time, it's a great way for lonely people to communicate. It can provide a voice for the voiceless and create communities of people who have shared interests and values. During times of isolation and desperation, that glowing screen can be the link for people who feel that no one is listening.

Loneliness is one of the afflictions of modern life and this was brought into focus during the pandemic, when people suddenly realised that there were neighbours in their streets who lived alone and had no one to support them.

Most commonly when we think of a lonely person, we imagine someone who is old and sad, when in real life that is often not the case. We can feel both happy and lonely, we can be young and feel lonely, we can hold down a full-time job and have a family and friends and feel lonely. Often, we don't want to say anything for fear of embarrassing ourselves or other people. Sometimes people don't want to say they're lonely or they don't want it pointed out to them. There is a charity called Marmalade which gives plenty of advice and support on loneliness, but empathy and kindness are vital.

The digital age has changed much about how we interact with each other and what makes us happy.

Some would argue that spirituality is harder to achieve in the world we live in now, but I disagree. I think that the far-reaching and unavoidable technology that we are plugged into and carry around in our pockets now just means we have to find new ways of allowing spirituality into our lives.

We live in a world where everything is instant. We expect instant gratification and then confuse that for happiness. So perhaps it's time to go back to basics and slow things down. When we get that urge to scroll through Instagram because we think that makes us happy, stop, breathe, do something else that makes you happy. Sing a song!

Technology has a role. It allows connection. When doing a reading on Zoom or Skype or whatever, I can still plug into the spirit energy, it's just as valid because it's just me and that person. The technology is just a tool, it's not the reason for the happiness and love that person feels: that comes from the spirit energy.

Happiness is one of the emotions that crosses the divide when we die. Along with love, it goes with our spirit energy. I can say this with confidence because when I pick up the energy of those in spirit, I can feel their happiness and often piggyback on it because it is infectious. There have been many times over the years when I've been preparing to go on stage and something has been rankling me and making me unhappy. But once the energy starts flowing, I can't help but feel elated and happy, even when some of the subject matter I deal with is sad. I'm lifted because their personalities and happiness shine through.

They often come through with a sense of humour and a joke too. They like to be mischievous and play pranks. One of my very first vivid experiences of spirit when I was young involved a ghost trying to trick me. I had a record player and had just bought a new single with my pocket money. I think it was an early Cliff Richard track. As I was playing it, and probably singing in the mirror holding a hairbrush as a microphone, I heard a man shout, "Shut that bloody racket up!" It filled the whole room. It was our resident ghost having a laugh, trying to make me jump.

There are people who perhaps have a more muted sense of humour, and who would class themselves as pessimists and introverts. Are they any less spiritual because of this? The answer is no, because while spirit energy loves laughter, real happiness doesn't have to manifest itself in laughter and jokes and gregariousness. People can be happy through contentment, love, self-esteem and self-worth. And all these things can be developed and learned. We are not automatically born with a sense of humour, for example, although interestingly we are all born with an innate ability to laugh, as are many animals. Apes laugh, and a recent study found that human babies laugh more like apes than adults, making laughter sounds in the inhalation, as in primates, rather than the exhalation, as in adult humans. They learn to laugh like humans as they grow older.

We pass our sense of humour on to our children. I have my mother to thank for my independence, work ethic and sense of fun. I was lucky because she was young and very independent when I was growing up. She was really the breadwinner in our house, which was unusual in those days, but consequently, when I became an adult, I had the drive to work and earn my own money. My dad was a plumber. In those days, you had a seven-year apprenticeship to do the job and he always seemed to be on his apprenticeship and never quite qualified fully. That's what he said, anyway. Now I'm older and wiser I suspect he wasn't a very good plumber and that was the reason why he never earned any money. My mum was the one that went out and worked, so it was instilled in me, especially as I was the oldest, that a woman can do anything.

When I think about it now, my mum was quite incredible. She was a woman beyond her time. She didn't know that, of course. She was simply trying to make ends meet and put food on the table. She was stunning and she could hypnotise men with her looks. She didn't take any crap from people, either. She ran a London probation service for 20 years, in which she would have been dealing with all kinds of male attitudes. She also worked for a pie company and set up their first customer services department, which mainly involved dealing with spurious complaints. She didn't intend to, but she'd been working as a secretary and answered a call from someone complaining about the amount of meat in a pie. She handled it so well, the boss gave her the responsibility of setting up the department. She'd come home and make us laugh, telling us about some of the tricks people would try, like putting a dead mouse in a pie and claiming that's how they bought it.

Nowadays, she probably would have been a politician or a CEO, but in those days the best an ambitious smart woman could hope for was to be spotted and given a more senior role that your male boss didn't fancy doing himself.

Subliminally, she passed on values to me that have stood me in good stead. She taught me that work can bring contentment and that everyone has ability and potential. That's why whenever I speak to people who tell me they are sad because they feel they have never fulfilled their potential, and they perhaps blame others for what they see as their failings in life, I explain that it's never too late, and that sometimes, life shows us the way.

It is within us to make our own happiness. Life doesn't always go to plan (which is why you should never plan too meticulously, too far ahead). And when things do go sideways, the things that will get you through are positivity and a sense of humour. With these in your toolkit, you often find happiness even in adversity, and even if you don't find happiness, you'll definitely find a way out of your predicament.

Chapter 11

Awakenings

The lady on the screen in front of me blinked back tears as soon as I mentioned the name that had just pinged into my mind with all the brightness and clarity of a light being switched on.

"Mark," I said. I knew he was in spirit.

I felt my chest tighten and a sensation of something being placed over my mouth. I'd done enough of these kind of readings by now to know what it meant.

"I'm so sorry," I said to the lady. "It was the virus, wasn't it?"

"He died two months ago," she explained.

"Well, he's here for you now," I smiled.

I could sense from Mark's energy that he was a fit man in his fifties and he was surprised to be where he was, in the afterlife.

I tried to make sense of the situation for his wife.

"You know, there was no rhyme or reason why it affected him the way it did. They haven't been able to work it out, why some people hardly had any symptoms and why others were so ill," I told her.

Mark was desperate for his wife to know that he hadn't suffered at the end. Like so many deaths during the pandemic, Mark had died without his wife at his side.

I saw a scene of a man in a hospital bed, intubated on a ventilator with an iPad propped on a stand next to him. On the screen was the same face on the screen in front of me.

"It was so hard, not being with him, wasn't it? But it was very peaceful when he passed," I explained. She had to say her goodbyes virtually. The cruelness of the situation was almost intolerable.

But the lady allowed herself a small, sad smile. It was small comfort knowing that her beloved husband was at peace and no longer suffering.

And then I felt a presence with Mark, a small child. And I saw him mouth the name Samuel.

"Did you have a baby in spirit?" I frowned. "He's saying Samuel."

Fresh tears sprung to the lady's eyes and she nodded, yes. I could sense that their child had died many years before. The energy between the spirit of the baby and its mother felt strong and full of love.

I saw another image in my mind. The lady was home, she was in front of a screen on which was the image of Mark in hospital. And around her, I could see the glow of her baby's energy.

"Samuel was there with you that night," I said. "He was protecting you and he was there for his dad when he passed. They're together now."

"I knew he was," the lady said. "I felt him with me. I never believed in anything like this, but it was so real I had to find out."

She had found her spiritual awakening.

Mine happened when I was four. I remember very clearly around the age I started nursery I began to realise I was different. Before that there were lots of little incidents, but they were fleeting. After the age of four, as my awareness of this world and the world beyond grew, I started on a journey of spiritual discovery. Of course I didn't know it at the time; I just thought the feelings I had and the images and sounds that inexplicably filled my mind were a part of me.

It's taken me all my life to analyse what's happening when I connect to spirit. It's taken decades of thought and experience to work out why it happens and how it happens. But I reckon by now, I've deciphered some of the truth. And as I explained earlier, science isn't a million miles away either.

Energy is the key to all life on this planet and to forces in the universe. Most of the energy we capture for use on Earth originates in the nuclear reactions powering our sun. This energy nourishes our planet and creates life; without it we wouldn't be here. It fuels everything and it resides in us all.

It is my belief that spiritual energy is another form of multi-dimensional energy that sits alongside, but separate, to the forms of energy we currently know about from physics, such as electricity and nuclear energy. It is, for now, unseen and illusive.

This energy resides in us all and reacts to our behaviours. It's enhanced and heightened by things like love and kindness and the other keys explained in this book. We can all enhance our spiritual energy, thereby increasing our spiritual capital. As a result, we become more spiritual ourselves.

In addition to the behaviours I've described, your spiritual journey starts by listening to what your spiritual energy is telling you. That means listening to your instincts and trusting your intuition. When you open yourself up to the possibilities of spirit energy, you will start to recognise the signs all around you and realise that the strange occurrences that you used to put down to coincidence, or dreams, or premonition, are real signs from energies beyond this world, gently telling you that there is so much more to life and death than what we think we know.

It takes practice and belief to be able to tune in to the spirit energy that pulses all around us and even more conviction to get to the point where you can start to understand the information within it. But as I hope I've shown you, if you want to open yourself up to the world of spirit energy and maybe sense the spirits of loved ones or be more aware and in tune with your own spirituality, there are ways you can develop it. At the end of this book, I have given you some exercises you can try to help you along the way.

It must start from within you. It's about trusting your gut feeling. It's about recognising when you get an intuitive feeling, trusting it and acting on it. It's about learning to know what those intuitive feelings are. It is not about a belief system. It is about trusting in the signs that are all around you. Why not a white feather? Why not a robin? Why not a smell or a touch? It is about trusting that those gut feelings you have when you see or experience something you think may have a hidden meaning, actually is what you subconsciously feel it is. If you give that credence, the energy it is connected to will connect with your energy.

Sadly, there are many elements on the Earth plane which stop us from developing and trusting these feelings. As adults we tend to pass doubts and scepticism to children who are born with purer energy. When they play with invisible friends, we tell them not to be so silly and to grow up. We tend to kill off their connection to their energy with kindness.

But things are changing. Spirituality is back in vogue and attitudes to it are changing. Everyone wants to be spiritual and to invite more spirituality into their lives. This doesn't mean simply posting inspiring messages on Facebook, or twisting into yoga poses for Instagram shots, while trying your best to keep a serene look on your face.

Spirituality has become an industry and much of it is inauthentic. There are fakes and faux gurus, happy to take your cash or your clicks and provide empty wisdom. If you are on a spiritual journey, you will encounter plenty of charlatans, but if you use the values and behaviours I've explained in these pages, you'll be guided and shown which are genuine and which are not. Again, it boils down to your intuition.

Thankfully there are good practitioners out there doing very good and worthwhile work, be they mediums, spiritualists, tarot readers or religious leaders. Reliable teachers and practitioners will have their own set of ethics and should be able to tell you about themselves and their work and why they are qualified to give you advice and guidance. You should question their motives, trust your instincts and look for word of mouth and recommendation.

Your curiosity may lead you to a medium, to someone like me. Many modern psychics have websites and they often give a flavour of what you can expect. If someone has a website that looks professional and well designed, rather than thrown together, this would usually suggest they have invested in their gift and are serious about it.

It is also worth taking into account how long a psychic has been practising professionally. If someone has been a full-time psychic for 20 or 30 years, the chances are they have been successful and are consequently decent and genuine.

Rather than relying on Google, I would recommend getting in contact with your nearest Spiritualist church and asking them. It doesn't matter if you are religious or believe in Spiritualism as a religion; they should be able to help as there will be people within the church who work as mediums and do private sittings.

Another reputable avenue to go down is the College of Psychic Studies which is based in London and was founded 125 years ago by a group of scholars and scientists. Its purpose was to facilitate formal investigation into the psychics and mediums that were at the centre of such popularity and debate in the Victoria era. They have a lot of good mediums there.

But before you even start looking for a medium, I would suggest that you think about the reasons you want to visit one.

There are usually two: curiosity, and the desire to contact someone specific in spirit. Both are valid reasons, and a bad experience can damage any future urges you may have to see other mediums. At its worst, a bad experience can leave you with doubt that the afterlife and spirit energy exists at all. If this happens to you, please remember it is not the world of spirit that is the problem, it is the medium. If your reasons are mercenary and self-serving, if you want to know whether you will be famous or how to get rich, you will never be satisfied, because you will not get the answers you want to hear. Spirit energy enriches the soul, not the pocket. I am certain of this because I've never been shown the winning lottery numbers or the winner of the 3:15 at Sandown. Spirit energy just doesn't work in that way.

Secret Spirit

Finally, the best way to judge a medium is through their accuracy. That is the benchmark. How accurate are they? How many hits do they get? It does help to be a nice person, but without accuracy you will not succeed as a professional medium. You need a good bedside manner, but it is no good to anyone if you are getting things wrong.

In all honesty, it is hard to find a good medium who has all of the attributes – accuracy, kindness, approachability, sense of humour, experience, empathy.

As a reader of this book, your spiritual journey is beginning. You are discovering the secrets within you that will connect you to a new level of energy. The time is right for your journey. The world has changed massively since we first learned of a novel virus affecting people in a far-off Chinese city that most of us had never heard of. What followed was not just a disease of the body. It affected the spirit, too. Millions lost loved ones, millions lost faith. Despair, desperation and disinformation are symptoms, too. But slowly the world is recovering.

Thanks to the wonders of human ingenuity and science, the sun is beginning to rise again after some very dark times, and with it comes a spiritual awakening. A new dawn. A new age of spirituality made possible by all the good that comes from the bad. The universal balance, an age-old law, says that after bad comes good, after dark comes light. There is a lot to be positive about following the global emergency we've been through. It might not always seem so, but the world worked together to develop treatments and vaccines. Scientists shared information, governments shared medication, the global community understood that we can only defeat the virus as a whole, rather than as single nations. Meanwhile communities pulled together to protect their vulnerable, and individuals showed remarkable acts of kindness and compassion.

Perhaps most profoundly, the virus made many re-evaluate what's important in life and reminded others that there are bigger priorities than material success. Nurses, teachers and checkout workers became heroes. They always were, of course; it just took the pandemic to remind us.

Many people were living spiritually bereft lives but never realised. They suffered a sickness of soul so deeply ingrained it became normal. The symptoms were a dull nagging sense that something wasn't quite right in life and a sense of emptiness. How many people went on that constant quest for gratification through material gain, but could never find satisfaction? I like to believe that, just maybe, as we come out of the pandemic, people will have a deeper sense of their core spirit and understand that fulfilment comes from within us, not from within a Chanel boutique. Maybe I'm just being a hopeless optimist! But I don't think I am. Something spiritual happened in the pandemic. How do you explain the astounding global outpouring of kindness and goodwill directed to a proud old man who decided to walk up and down his garden to raise money for the NHS? Captain Tom was riding the wave of spiritual energy sent out by thousands of well-wishers, and he was just one example of the incredible stories that became the human narrative of the pandemic.

Love is the key. It is the oil that lubricates the links between our world and the next. Love has everything to do with spirit because love nourishes energy. When spirits show themselves, it is to send us signs of love in times of need or turmoil. They come to guide us and to offer us support. Sometimes in the middle of our darkest times they swoop in to save us. Incredible things can happen when spirit energy is allowed to flow.

Exercises

It is a good idea to keep a spiritual journal, which can just be a notepad, in which you keep any ideas, do any exercises or jot down a record of your experiences or thoughts.

Define your reasons

A task that helps you to set your focus and purpose as you set out on your journey. Simply ask yourself why you want to develop your spiritual energy. Are you doing it for well-being? Do you want to use your spirituality for the good of others? Are you keen to link to anyone who has passed?

Write down your answers in your journal and refer back to them from time to time.

Calm mind, open senses

This can be practised daily for you to begin to trust in your spirituality and awaken your energy. Sit quietly and reflect on the stimuli you feel and the thoughts in your head. Do not force them. Try to let your mind wander automatically. Reflect on how you feel.

What images come into your mind?

Do you sense any smells or feelings?

Automatic writing

Gently rest a pencil on a blank sheet of A4 paper. Look away or close your eyes and let your hand move, but do not consciously write. It takes practice, and sometimes it helps to ask questions that you might want guidance for.

See if your hand starts to produce words or images.

Spotting signs

Spirit energy doesn't give straightforward information. It talks to us in dreams, or sends us signs and symbols that come in many forms, such as a white feather, a robin, a butterfly, a smell, a sound, music, a touch, a thought or feeling that seems out of place. Practise watching out for these and working out their significance.

For example, you may have been thinking of someone and then hear a piece of music you associate with them. Or they may even call or text. Note these signs down so you have a record. The more spiritual you become, the more you will notice them.

Practise psychometry

Psychometry is a form of extrasensory perception, whereby a person can draw information from an object by making physical contact with it. Practise this with an object you can borrow from someone you know and which is sentimental to them.

Clear your mind and begin to practise the calm mind open senses techniques discussed previously. Feel yourself relaxing and your mind clearing.

Pick up the object and hold it gently in your hands. Look at the object with a clear mind and focus on the person who owns it. Try to feel their energy surrounding you. Thoughts will pop into your head. No matter how random they may feel to you, write these thoughts, words and images down. Remember, something that makes no sense to you may make complete sense to the person. Tell them what you noted and see if makes any sense to them.

Now practise with an object which you are unfamiliar with, but that is also likely to hold a store of spirit energy, such as a piece of jewellery or a photo. You could pick such an item up cheaply at a car boot sale or a charity shop. Hold it and make a note of what you see and feel in your mind.

Do you see any images, feel emotions, hear sounds or receive smells and tastes?

Try to see if you can discover who owned the object. What was their personality?

What words pop into your mind?

What sensations do you feel?

Create your spiritual happy place

Close your eyes and breathe deeply and slowly.

Imagine a place where you feel safe and happy. This can be somewhere you know or an imaginary place.

Start to layer your senses in this place. What does it feel like, what are the sounds, what do you see, what are the smells?

Who is there with you?

Build this place in your mind. It could be your favourite beach, it could be a warm bath, it could simply be on a cosy sofa with the person you love. Really enrich your mental imagery and practise going to this place frequently. The more you conjure it up, the easier you will find it to create this place when you need to be calm, feel safe or just relax.

Create your future

The future can be whatever you want it to be, whether you want to start your own business, find love, get fit or live a meaningful life. Reflect on what you want and imagine it. Write it down. Imagine reaching that stage in life.

Frequently return to these thoughts and aspirations to set your purpose.

Meditate

Find somewhere quiet and comfortable where you will not be disturbed and sit on a comfortable chair or sit cross-legged on a cushion if this is comfortable.

Close your eyes and take deep breaths. Focus on the inhalation and exhalation. Try to imagine your chest expanding and contracting gently with each breath.

Listen to the sound the breath makes and focus on it. Try not to think of anything but the breath and the way it makes your body move as your lungs fill and your diaphragm rises and falls.

Your mind will naturally wander and thoughts will enter your head. When they do, acknowledge them but don't expand on them or follow them, just allow them to pass, bringing your attention and focus back to the breath.

You will also notice physical things, perhaps from the way you are sitting. Acknowledge them, observe, but then bring your focus back to your breath. In this way you will begin to see your conscious thoughts drift past like clouds in the sky, while you serenely observe them.

Practise empathy

When you are on a bus or train or in a waiting room, focus on a stranger (don't stare, just observe). Notice their mannerisms, expressions and behaviours and start to read them.

What are they feeling, are they happy or sad?

What kind of personality do they have?

Try to see the situation they are in from their perspective. Are they near a window and too cold?

Is someone near them annoying them?

The aim of this exercise is to try to feel what they may be feeling.

Practise kindness

This exercise requires some honesty. Let's face it, we all have people in our lives that annoy us from time to time. That's just human nature. Focus on that individual and on the things about them that annoy you, or maybe the things they've done that have upset you.

Now try to see their behaviour from their perspective.

The object of this exercise is to reach an understanding of why you find them annoying. What are the reasons behind their behaviour?

Have you done something to them to make them act the way they do?

Can you reach a place from where you can start to understand why they are the way they are?

No one is inherently bad and there are always reasons why people are the way they are. Did you know for example that bullies were often bullied themselves?

Forgive someone

Think of someone you could forgive, perhaps a former lover who cheated on you, or a parent who you feel let you down. Write them a letter in which you explain that you understand why they did what they did and that you forgive them.

You can choose to send the letter or not, but in your heart, find the love to forgive them. This exercise also works the other way round. If you have done something for which you want to be forgiven, ask for that forgiveness.

Make a happiness list

Write down five things that make you happy, but that don't include money or possessions. These could be your children, sunshine, laughter, a walk in the park.

Whenever you need reminding that life is good, look at your list and connect with it.

Then do something that makes you happy.

Write a bucket list

It's always baffled me why people often leave bucket lists until it's too late. You shouldn't wait until you're dying to do the things you've always wanted. Write your bucket list and try to tick a few things off each year.

Acknowledgements

Thank you to friends and family for your continued love and energy.

Thank you to all at Mardle Books for allowing me to share these teachings and thank you to Nick for all your help.

Useful contacts

Samaritans
www.samaritans.org
Helpline 116 123

Campaign Against Living Miserably (CALM)
www.thecalmzone.net
0800 585858

The Spiritualist Association of Great Britain
www.sagb.org.uk/

MIND
www.mind.org.uk/
0300 123 3393

Marmalade Trust
www.marmaladetrust.org

Cruse Bereavement Care
www.cruse.org.uk
0808 808 1677

At a loss
www.ataloss.org

Widowed and Young
www.widowedandyoung.org.uk

Child Bereavement UK
www.childbereavementuk.org
0800 02 888 40